STRANGE STORIES

A Compendium of the True, the Untrue, and the Definitively Maybe

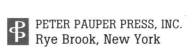

PETER PAUPER PRESS, INC.
Rye Brook, New York

PETER PAUPER PRESS

In 1928, at the age of twenty-two, Peter Beilenson began printing books on a small press in the basement of his parents' home in Larchmont, New York. Peter—and later, his wife, Edna—sought to create fine books that sold at "prices even a pauper could afford."

Today, still family owned and operated, Peter Pauper Press continues to honor our founders' legacy of quality, value, and fun for big kids and small kids alike.

By Hannah Beilenson, Matthew Cosgrove, T. Levy,
Sarah Longstreth, and Virginia Reynolds

Designed by Heather Zschock
Images used under license from Shutterstock.com, courtesy of Creative Market,
and used under Creative Commons licenses. For additional credits, see page 129.

Special thanks to Jacob, Vayda, Sarah, Izzy, Roy,
and Oren for sharing all their strange knowledge with us.

Copyright © 2024 Peter Pauper Press, Inc.
3 International Drive
Rye Brook, NY 10573 USA

Published in the United Kingdom and Europe by
Peter Pauper Press, Inc. c/o White Pebble International
Units 2-3, Spring Business Park
Stanbridge Road
Havant, Hampshire PO9 2GJ, UK

Library of Congress Control Number: 2024931508

While our editors have worked to ensure the accuracy of the stories presented here, please note that in light of changing information and circumstances, there may be unintentional inaccuracies or omissions. We encourage you to use this book as a springboard for exploration, and to verify facts independently.

www.peterpauper.com

STRANGE STORIES

CONTENTS

GREAT MICHIGAN PIZZA FUNERAL

On March 5, 1973, Mario Fabbrini ceremoniously buried 29,188 frozen pizzas before a crowd of several hundred onlookers and one Michigan governor William Milliken. On the pizzas' grave, Fabbrini placed a wreath of red and white flowers, the color of a beautiful, cheesy slice.

Why the funeral? Well, one of Fabbrini's suppliers suspected that some canned mushrooms they sent him were contaminated with botulism, a rare bacteria that can cause deadly food poisoning. When the Food and Drug Administration heard about this, they immediately ordered that the pizzas be recalled. But Fabbrini made lemonade out of lemons, or in this case, publicity out of a botulism scare, and used the funeral for some helpful exposure.

At the time, Fabbrini's factory employed twenty-two people, and could produce 45,000 pizzas every week. By recalling just under 30,000 pizzas from production, Fabbrini worried about the loss of profit—after all, his food *was* popular—but he also worried about his reputation. Now people might forever associate his delicious pizza with botulism. By burying the pizzas, he was not only able to gain the upper hand in the media narratives swirling around, but also to send consumers a clear message: "I will not poison your pizza, America." To hammer the point home, he served (mushroom-free) pizza at the event.

However, tragedy was on the horizon. The deceased pizzas may have been innocent after all. Fabbrini agreed to toss the pizzas when two laboratory mice died after eating his product. But weeks after the pizzas were mourned and buried, it was determined that the mice didn't die of botulism. Fabbrini commented, "I think it was indigestion. . . . Maybe they did not like my pizzas."

Fabbrini watches over the pizza burial

Fabbrini sued the companies that canned and sold the mushrooms, and was awarded $211,000 (worth more than $1.4 million today) by the Michigan Court of Appeals—more than making up the estimated $60,000 worth of pizza he buried.

Let's all raise a slice.

RI PIZZA

THE INCREDIBLE SILKWORM CAPER

Two Byzantine monks are traveling home after a lengthy journey, likely making their way along the Black Sea. It's been a long, strange trip since they first set out to China around 552 CE. They've traveled hundreds if not thousands of miles. They've packed light for the return trip, taking only the meager supplies they need on the long trek itself. And though they're returning from China, home to many of the world's most valuable trade goods, they do not bring back wagons full of spices and gems. No. They have a few canes of bamboo and some potted mulberry bushes, likely given as gifts to the poor, humble brothers.

These monks were in fact pulling off the heist of the millennium, though nobody who crossed paths with them would have suspected it. Those bamboo canes were stuffed with wriggly larvae. The monks were smuggling silkworm eggs back to the Byzantine Empire, acting under the direct orders of Emperor Justinian I. This early act of industrial espionage would change the face of the world for centuries to come.

The monks had first been to China some years earlier, on their way back from preaching in India. During their trip, they observed the intricacies of silk production—an incredibly delicate process revolving around the humble silkworm, and a complete mystery back home.

China had a monopoly on silk-making, and had since at least 3600 BCE. Woven silk fabric was a luxury good of the highest quality, and the rest of the

world was enamored with it. But the secrets of precisely *how* silk was produced and woven remained closely guarded. By the time Justinian I took the throne, importing silk was more expensive and difficult than ever, while demand remained high. So when a group of monks reported a way for the empire to bypass their trade partners and get some silk right from the source, Justinian saw an opportunity too good to pass up.

The plan had to be flawless. Simply stealing a few eggs wouldn't cut it. Without their favorite food, the silkworms would all die long before they made any silk. The mulberry plants that the monks brought back, seemingly as souvenirs, were just as crucial to their success as the hidden eggs. Baby silkworm larvae eat mulberry leaves and *only* mulberry leaves. After eating truly huge amounts of the plant, and molting four whole times, the worms pupate and spin their silken cocoons. The cocoons' fragile fibers must then be carefully processed before being unwound and spun into silken thread.

Emperor Justinian Receiving the First Imported Silkworm Eggs from Nestorian Monks

The result of Justinian's plot? A flourishing silk industry in the Byzantine Empire, and a ready source of the luxury fabric for their many trading partners in what then made up the western world. The Silk Road to China still thrived, and Chinese silk remained at a premium value. Westerners still needed to be pretty rich to wear silk, too, but the new monopoly made it a bit easier to get your hands on it if you weren't the most upper-crust royalty. Byzantine silk became both a trade good worth its weight in gold, and a powerful diplomatic gift to new allies.

What we don't know is what became of the monks who changed the world economy with their wormy bamboo. Were they rewarded for their daring? Did they quietly retire? How much did they even benefit from the trade they helped create? Maybe the real priceless treasure was the friends they made along the way.

DO BOOKSTORES CONTROL OUR BATHROOM HABITS?

In 1985, a woman named Mariko Aoki had a question she needed answered desperately, so she wrote to the Japanese magazine *Hon no Zasshi* with just one thing on her mind: Why does she always have to poop when she goes to a bookstore?

If you've ever had this feeling yourself, you're not alone. The sudden urge to defecate in bookstores is now called the **Mariko Aoki phenomenon**, after the woman who infamously wrote about the experience. Following her letter, reports from readers with similar problems poured in.

People have since speculated if the effect is real, and what the cause could be. Which of these three theories do you think is most likely?

1. There are chemicals in paper that make you have to poop when you smell it—a grand conspiracy designed to make you use toilet paper faster.

2. People associate bookstores with reading on the toilet, which people have been doing for a long time. Back in the 1700s, people kept newspapers, almanacs, and cheap books close at hand, to wipe with after reading. Before you judge, remember, people in America didn't have modern toilet paper until 1857.

3.

Mariko Aoki was just weird. But hey, aren't we all?

No matter what's really behind the Mariko Aoki effect, we've learned one thing for sure: don't tell a magazine about your odd poop habit if you don't want it named after you.

Speaking of toilets, did you know that the rise of public restrooms in the USA can be traced all the way back to Prohibition? In the early twentieth century, most of the toilets people could find in American cities were either in hotels, department stores, or saloons. The stores and hotels weren't accessible to everyone, and saloons—remembered today mainly as the setting of old cowboy movie showdowns—didn't mesh well with the values of some policymakers at the time. When the Eighteenth Amendment outlawed alcohol in 1920, and saloons had to close by the thousands, people had more reason than ever to demand safe public places to pee.

This toilet will be remembered forever—can you spot it?

We take public toilets for granted today, but the arrival of indoor plumbing was a big deal in Victorian England. In the 1850s, after the country's first flush toilet was unveiled, Oxford University's Christ Church Cathedral installed a new stained-glass window depicting a toilet.

13

EMPRESS CATHERINE'S NEED FOR SPEED

Picture this: against the wintry backdrop of Russian palaces, a giant wooden sled speeds down the snowy hills, carrying a group of delighted passengers whose shrieks echo across the landscape. What you are envisioning is no tourist attraction—in the eighteenth century, only the esteemed friends and guests of Empress Catherine the Great were permitted to climb the 70-foot (21 m) wooden tower and slide down hundreds of feet of ice at speeds your average peasant wouldn't even dream of.

Winters in Russia are long, but they don't last forever, so there was a time limit on how many thrills Catherine and friends could experience each year before the event was packed up for warmer weather. Catherine felt the approaching spring near and found it unacceptable. So she did what any innovator (with unlimited funds, resources, and time) would do. She commissioned the first ever roller coaster.

Catherine's model shared much in common with the original icy slide—it still made use of a wooden ramp and the natural infrastructure of the Russian landscape. But in order to achieve high speeds in summer months, she had wheels added to the carts (which were carved like lavish chariots, *of course*) and hired elite architects to build five wavy wooden tracks down the mountain. She also decided that the original slide wasn't nearly long enough. Her roller coaster rolled for more than 1600 feet (500 m)—the distance of about four and a half football fields. The carts went faster the more passengers they had, and at high enough speeds, riders could fly down all five tracks. When the ride was finished, a team of horses brought the carts back to their starting place.

The Aerial Walk

Not long after this, the French put their own spin on the concept. In 1817, the Promenades-Aériennes (or "The Aerial Walk") debuted in Paris. On tracks with grooves down the middle, passengers rode sideways-facing benches at speeds of 40 miles per hour (60 km/h).

Eventually, roller coasters would welcome all guests, not just royal ones. But the amusement park that housed the Aerial Walk was also geared toward the upper crust of France. Even King Louis XVIII visited the park and marveled at the Aerial Walk. However, we have no record of whether or not he actually tried the ride—not everyone sought out thrills like Catherine.

If you want to try something a little less fancy and proper than Louis XVIII might show up to, you can go to BonBon-Land, a candy-themed amusement park in Denmark, and ride the *Hundeprutterutchebane*, Danish for "Dog-Fart Roller Coaster." Hop on the ride and travel past a sculpture of a friendly dog mid-poop while surround-sound speakers bark and make fart noises. Sure, eighteenth-century aristocrats might not like it, but they also didn't have tap water, so what do they know about fun?

HOUDINI'S LAST HALLOWEEN

He was buried alive. Locked in an oversized milk can. Nailed into a packing crate and lowered into the East River. Sealed

inside a boiler. Suspended upside down in a tank of water. And each time, as throngs of people gathered to watch, Harry Houdini freed himself and defied death. But one Halloween, he would not be so lucky.

Today, Harry Houdini is remembered for his countless feats as a magician and escape artist. He first performed as a trapeze artist at the age of nine, but soon became enamored with the art of stage magic, especially escape acts.

Houdini traveled the vaudeville circuit all around the USA, amazing crowds with his ability to break out of handcuffs, straitjackets, padlocked chains, and more. It wasn't long before his stunts became enormous spectacles, drawing tens of thousands of onlookers. He toured Great Britain, the Netherlands, France, Russia, and Germany, challenging local police to handcuff him and lock him up in jail cells. Each time, police would thoroughly search Houdini before placing him behind iron bars. And each time, Houdini would escape.

Because his acts required such incredible strength and finesse, Houdini considered his fitness to be the basis of his success as a performer. "My muscles are absolutely under my control at every moment," he wrote, in a 1924 fitness advice column for the *Tampa Sunday Tribune*. "If I should, for an instant, lose my muscular control, I should be lost—my life might be the price I'd have to pay."

Perhaps he did.

In October 1926, Houdini was booked for a show at the Princess Theater in Montreal, Canada. Despite breaking his ankle during an underwater escape in New York a few days earlier, he kept the gig and even made time to give a lecture at McGill University on fraudulent spirit mediums. Debunking these psychic scammers was a major focus of Houdini's later years; he often showed up at seances in disguise, accompanied by police and reporters, to expose how these performers took advantage of vulnerable, grieving people.

After the lecture, Houdini allowed a few admirers to visit him back at the theater, where they witnessed a fateful event. According to one account, the visiting students saw Houdini lying on his side (broken ankle, remember?), reading some mail and posing for a sketch. When a man named Jocelyn Gordon Whitehead asked if it was true his stomach muscles could withstand any punch, Houdini "remarked rather unenthusiastically" that they could resist quite a bit. Whitehead decided to put this to the test, and punched Houdini hard below the belt. Houdini winced and stopped Whitehead after several strikes, saying he had not had time to prepare for the punches and that his injury prevented him from moving to a safe position.

A normal Tuesday for Harry Houdini.

The Houdinis in 1913

Houdini's stomach hurt worse and worse over the course of the evening, but he went on with the show. Two days later, sleepless from the pain but determined to begin a two-week engagement in Detroit, he was examined by a doctor in his dressing room and diagnosed with acute appendicitis. The doctor insisted he go to the hospital at once, but Houdini had a show to perform. He struggled through the performance, finally went to the hospital afterward, and died a week later, on Halloween.

Although Houdini debunked many sham mystics and mediums, he still remained curious about the afterlife. Before he died, Houdini gave his wife Bess a secret code. If he returned as a ghost, he would communicate this message to her as proof that spirits really could continue on.

Bess held seances every year on Halloween, but never received the message (which was "Rosabelle Believe," a reference to the couple's favorite song). To this day, it is a tradition for some magicians to hold a Halloween seance for Houdini, hoping to get a glimpse of the master of magic.

THE GREATEST INVENTION SINCE, WELL, EVER

If you still hear people call stuff "the greatest thing since sliced bread," it's probably because the novelty hasn't worn off yet. We've only been buying it pre-sliced for about a century—actually, since 1928. So what baker devised the convenient loaves we use for sandwiches, French toast, and fairy bread?

Well, it wasn't a baker at all, but a jeweler named Otto Rohwedder, who knew almost zilch about bread but quite a bit about delicate machinery. The mechanical blades of his invention produced even, consistent slices that were each just under half an inch (1 cm). Bakers at the time thought it was a terrible idea, worrying that pre-sliced loaves would quickly go stale. But Rohwedder took a risk and partnered with an old friend, Frank Bench, who owned a bakery in Chillicothe, Missouri. To garner interest in the invention, the two took out an ad in the local paper, reassuring readers that although "the idea of sliced bread may be startling to some people," they would inevitably come to realize it was "sound, sensible, and in every way a progressive refinement" in the world of bread.

Rohwedder's bread slicer in action

Within two weeks, sales at Bench's bakery skyrocketed, and it wasn't long before sliced bread took over grocery shelves all over America. The invention also popularized the automatic toaster—uniform slices made the toaster more effective and easier to use.

Sliced bread was here to stay. There was a dip during World War II, when rationing efforts led to a brief, deeply unpopular ban on factory-sliced bread. *The New York Times* wrote that the ban caused consumers to risk "thumbs and tempers slicing bread at home," particularly given how hard it was to find a good bread knife. (Factories were using all their metal for the war, and had almost none left to make household items.) In less than fifteen years, sliced bread had become such a part of American life that citizens were stressed and even *hurt* without it. The ban was lifted after just two months, and a sigh of relief swept the nation.

The town of Chillicothe, Missouri, is pretty proud to be the hometown of this invention. If you ever visit, make sure to stop by the welcome center—it's hard to miss, just look for the building with a big loaf of bread on its roof. The state of Missouri also recognizes July 7 as Sliced Bread Day, in case you ever need an excuse to party.

CADAVER SYNOD: DEAD POPE ON TRIAL

The year was 897 CE, and Pope Formosus was on trial for perjury, ascending to the papacy illegally, and other pope stuff that was definitely against the rules. Pope Formosus didn't have a lawyer—no one had a lawyer in 897—but he had something even more troublesome working against him. *He was already dead.*

The trial was conducted by Pope Stephen VI, who had Formosus's corpse dug up and brought to court. Stephen was not the pope after Formosus, but the pope after the pope after Formosus. The pope in between was called Boniface IV, and he had lasted less than a month. (Keep that in mind for later.)

Formosus was found guilty, and Stephen declared his papacy invalid, but that's no surprise. You're not going to put a dead guy on trial if you're not convinced you can win. But why do this at all?

As it turns out, the answer is political. Becoming pope back then was complicated, and required a delicate balance of power and relationships with the right people. The pope got to pick the emperor, so it really mattered who became the pope. And lots of people wanted the job!

However, there were laws that forbid religious officials from openly campaigning to get the role, mostly because it was a lifetime gig. If you were *too* eager to be the new pope, it would look like you wanted the current guy dead. When Formosus was alive (and before he was the pope), he was a bishop, gaining power and popularity remarkably fast. John VIII, the pope at the time, didn't care for this, and had Formosus excommunicated (kicked out of the church).

A while after John VIII died—by murder, so he was right to be suspicious, although he'd blamed the wrong guy—Formosus was reinstated. And eventually, in 891, he was elected pope. He kept the position for five years until he passed away. Then Boniface became pope for a whopping fifteen days, and then we get to Pope Stephen VI.

Remember Stephen VI? The guy who sued a corpse? Turns out, the same laws he used against Formosus could also be used against him. By putting Formosus on trial, Pope Stephen VI was able to effectively distract from his own illegal activities—possibly including the murder of Boniface VI—because when you put the dead body of a pope on trial, no one can really think about anything else.

After Formosus was found guilty (because *obviously*), Pope Stephen VI had the body buried. Then he dug it back up and tossed it in a river, a dramatic gesture normally reserved for Rome's greatest enemies. Before long, the Roman public decided they'd had enough of this guy. He was overthrown and put in prison, where—you guessed it—he was murdered. His successor Romanus was pope for about a year, and spent a lot of that time annulling everything Stephen VI did. The next pope, Theodore II, managed an even more impressive feat in his mere twenty-day tenure: he found Formosus's body (well, a fisherman found him, because fishermen spend more time pulling things out of rivers than popes do) and ordered him reburied. He also held a new synod (pope meeting) to have Stephen's deeply weird "Cadaver Synod" overturned. Formosus's good name was finally returned to him, and he could rest with all the other former popes.

Just for good measure, the next pope, John IX, declared there would be no more dead-person trials allowed. Kind of messed up that anybody had to make a rule about it, but at least someone did. So . . . faith in justice restored? I guess??

Hey! I'm Thomas Edison, I invented the Kinetograph!

FIRST EVER CAT VIDEO

Imagine for a moment: the year is 1894, and you are Thomas Edison, inventor of the lightbulb and the phonograph, plus a bunch of other stuff people mostly won't remember in a hundred years, but you don't know that yet. Also, you love cats.

Movies don't exist yet, but that's okay, because you're Thomas Edison. So you invent a machine called the Kinetograph, an early motion-picture camera, and you take a twenty-second film of two cats in grainy black-and-white.

You obviously want to show off your new cinematic masterpiece, so you invent the Kinetoscope to go with it—a device that can show a

short film to a single viewer. (Your employee William Kennedy Laurie Dickson does most of the actual work on both machines, but like many a group-project slacker, you're happy to slap your own name on the patent. I mean, who has time to spell out "William Kennedy Laurie Dickson"? Might as well save everyone some time and just put "Thomas Edison.") When people line up one at a time to peer through your Kinetoscope's peephole window, they see a film of two cats pawing at each other with boxing gloves. They will also see you standing gleefully behind them, pulling back the furry fighters whenever the match gets too heated.

It's *so* cute, and in just over a century, people will post videos just like it to the internet, something you did *not* invent, but that's okay. Because sharing videos of cute cats is humanity's most important mission, and nothing will stand in its way.

CINÉMATOGRAPHE LUMIÈRE

So maybe you're thinking, "Okay, that's cool, but what was the first ever movie?"

To answer that, we have to skip forward about a year. Everyone has seen the Edison cats by this point, and they're tired of it. They're done with cats. We jump from America to Paris to find the Lumière brothers, Auguste and Louis, with their brand-new invention, the Cinématographe. On December 28, 1895, the two arranged a screening to showcase ten short films to an audience in Paris. Two of those films were *Workers Leaving the Lumière Factory*, a simple everyday scene that nonetheless caused a sensation, and *The Gardener*, the first known film comedy. (Later titled *L'Arroseur arrosé*, or "The Sprinkled Sprinkler," it features a boy pranking a gardener into spraying himself in the face with his hose. Honestly, it holds up.) The screening was a massive success, even though all ten films together only amounted to a twenty-minute runtime.

Want to hear about a movie that only exists in the internet's collective imagination? Check out page 61.

GENGHIS KHAN'S POSTAL SYSTEM

In the 1200s CE, the Mongol Empire covered the largest contiguous territory in history—more than 9 million square miles (24 million km) across Eurasia at its peak. Genghis Khan's empire is remembered for its uniquely powerful and advanced military strategies, and it oversaw a flourishing trade network that spanned the continent. But there's another important institution that the empire depended on: its postal system.

Messengers could use these paizas to travel safely through the empire.

Though not equipped with stamps, mailboxes, and fun uniforms, the Yam, a supply and postal route first established during the Great Khan's rule, proved invaluable to the empire. Genghis's successor Ögedei Khan expanded and strengthened the system, establishing Yam stations every 20 to 40 miles (32 to 54 km) across vast swaths of territory. Messengers arrived at each station to hand off messages to a new rider, then rest before their next delivery. Each station had everything you might need: food, a place to sleep, fresh horses—kind of like a bed and breakfast for post officers, if bed and breakfasts were guarded by about a thousand warriors.

This fast, reliable route allowed for information and intelligence to reach important figures quickly, giving

A Russian yamstchik in uniform

military groups time to respond to threats and unusual events. The system was so efficient that it was admired by travelers all over the world. Even after the empire declined, parts of the system remained. Tsarist Russia used the leftover stations for government communication and later for regular mail service. Postal workers in that era were called yamstchiks, after the Mongolian Yam.

Where in the World Is Genghis Khan's Dead Body?

Genghis Khan wanted to keep his death a complete secret. He had brought his army to stop a rebellion, and he knew the people trying to resist his empire would feel pretty good if they found out he died. So his heirs and followers obeyed his two last wishes: to destroy the enemy's cities immediately, and to go to great lengths to hide his resting place. The Khan's warriors killed any accidental witnesses to his funeral procession, and rode their thousand horses over his grave until no evidence remained. Legends hold that he is buried on top of a mountain, though it's not clear which one (or how you'd get a thousand horses up there). Most likely, the tomb is forever out of reach in the vast plains and peaks of Mongolia, just as the Khan intended.

EVERYTHING IS GOING GREAT FOR SALOMON AUGUST ANDRÉE

Salomon August Andrée and his two companions were in a tight spot. Their hydrogen balloon had crashed almost two months ago, and they were running out of supplies. The arctic island they were camping on was inhospitable and entirely deserted. Andrée remained optimistic in spite of the dire circumstances. His last journal entries described moments of their grueling, weeks-long trek across the ice floes as "Paradise!" and insisted that "Morale remains good."

Good morale or not, all three men were dead in short order. They perished more than 600 miles (1,000 km) south from their objective: the North Pole. Their bodies wouldn't be discovered for more than thirty years.

The general idea behind their expedition wasn't necessarily a bad one. Traveling to the North Pole by sea was an incredibly dangerous and difficult endeavor. Why not simply *fly* to the North Pole using a hydrogen balloon?

Okay, it's pretty clear that the general idea behind their expedition was a bad one, given what we know now. But Andrée, a Swedish engineer and balloonist, was convinced that such a scheme could work. With a properly constructed balloon, enough supplies, and some careful maneuvering, the North Pole was in reach!

The main problem with using a balloon for such a journey was obvious, even to Andrée: balloons were at the mercy of the winds. You couldn't steer a balloon as you might a boat. But Andrée had found a solution. By dragging long ropes behind the balloon, he had found that it was possible to control the direction of flight—not by much, but enough that he could steer at least a little. Good enough for him!

Andrée sought investors and publicity, and was hugely successful. The King of Sweden himself contributed funds, as did Alfred Nobel, the inventor of dynamite and namesake of the Nobel Prize. Andrée was a charismatic and persuasive speaker. He was optimistic that the journey could be accomplished with ease, that all of the conditions would be perfect for such an expedition, and that success was practically guaranteed.

But this optimism was perhaps a tad misplaced. A whole slew of problems arose. The balloon leaked—a lot. The arctic weather was far harsher than expected. And Andrée's drag-rope steering technique? Great in theory, but it didn't work. At all.

Whenever people brought up potential issues with the expedition, Andrée waved away their worries without bothering to investigate or fix them. One of his companions, an experienced arctic researcher in charge of pumping the hydrogen, observed that the balloon was leaking far too much to remain airborne for the planned thirty days of flight. Andrée said it was *fine*. No big deal.

The results were disastrous.

The balloon, the Eagle, took off from Norway's Svalbard archipelago in July of 1897. Almost immediately, the drag-ropes caught on some rocks and nearly sent everything crashing into the water. Most of the ropes detached and fell to the ground. The crew dumped ballast and successfully took off, but it was a worrying start. Once they were finally in the air, the three men settled in for the thirty days of gentle flight Andrée had promised.

The Eagle was down on the ice after only two days and three hours. Turns out the hydrogen leak *was* a big deal.

The expedition crew had been well prepared for their journey by air, but not at all prepared for a journey on foot over arctic ice floes. The sleds they loaded with supplies broke, and they were forced to abandon large amounts of food and equipment. They tried to travel back in the direction of Svalbard, but the drifting ice worked against them. Still, Andrée looked on the bright side, writing in his journal: "Paradise! Large, even ice floes with pools of sweet drinking water and here and there a tender-fleshed young polar bear!"

They made it off the ice and onto the island of Kvitøya, where they died of uncertain causes. (Theories have included hypothermia, exhaustion, undercooked bear meat, canned-food lead poisoning, and polar bear attack.) An unfortunate end for three people with great ambitions. Salomon August Andrée would have done well to learn a simple fact: hoping for the best is fine, but preparing for the worst could go a long way toward keeping you alive.

BENJAMIN FRANKLIN'S ELECTROCUTION BY TURKEY

When people think of Benjamin Franklin's experiments with electricity, they often imagine the famous kite incident. In the middle of a thunderstorm, Franklin and his son flew a kite to prove that lightning was, in fact, electric. A wire on the kite picked up ambient electricity from the storm, and the charge traveled down a hemp string to a metal key on the ground. When the key made an electric spark, Franklin knew he'd found the link. Eventually, this led to his creation of the lightning rod, which protects structures from lightning damage during storms.

Commendable! But this wasn't Franklin's first experiment with electricity. In fact, two years earlier, in 1750, he tried a different and somehow even more dangerous experiment.

Franklin believed electricity could lead to better-tasting meats. (The dinner-party spectacle of serving an electrocuted turkey, strung up in a mad-scientist array of wires and beakers, appealed to him as well.) One night, when trying to cook a turkey with two full jars of electrical charge, Benjamin Franklin accidentally shocked himself—badly. "In making these Experiments, I found that a Man can without great Detriment bear a much greater Electrical Shock than I imagin'd," he later wrote, capital letters and all. "It seemed a universal Blow from head to foot throughout the Body, and was follow'd by a violent quick Trembling in the Trunk, which wore gradually off in a few seconds." He said the sound of the shock was as loud as a pistol, and left a mark on his hand almost the size of a pistol wound, too. And although he was pleased to survive the experiment, he firmly described it as an experience "that I desire never **never** to repeat."

So, for reference, he did this, and then *two years later* flew a kite in the middle of a thunderstorm. To his credit, though, he took some precautions this time—holding the kite by a silk string that wouldn't draw electricity, and standing safely inside the door to avoid a direct lightning strike that would likely have killed him.

But how did the turkey taste? Well, according to Franklin, "uncommonly tender."

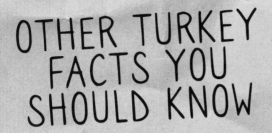

OTHER TURKEY FACTS YOU SHOULD KNOW

Male turkeys are called gobblers. The big, silly red sacks on their faces are the *snood* and the *wattle*.

Wild turkeys were almost hunted to extinction by the start of the twentieth century. (Benjamin Franklin, we hold you responsible.)

You can determine a turkey's gender by its droppings. Hen poops are spiral-shaped, and gobbler poops are shaped like a long letter J.

While We're Talking about Benjamin Franklin . . .

Before becoming a politician, before even becoming an adult, Benjamin Franklin was an excellent writer. When he was sixteen, his brother James founded a newspaper called the *New England Courant*. After James repeatedly said no to publishing his little brother's essays, Benjamin Franklin secretly submitted letters under the alias "Mrs. Silence Dogood," a forty-year-old widow. In the voice of the Widow Dogood, he wrote about various issues of colonial life, sharing thoughts on government, religion, virtue, and vice. He wrote fourteen letters total under this pseudonym (fooling James completely), and they were so popular that some men even sent Silence Dogood marriage proposals. What a catch!

HEAD LIKE A HOLE: PHINEAS GAGE

The explosion threw Phineas Gage through the air and onto his back. The other men feared the worst, but he woke within a few minutes and got to his feet, walking again with only a little assistance. He spoke without issue, which onlookers found surprising, since he had a gaping hole in his head. His brain was visible, and he was bleeding extensively. Still he remained awake, sitting upright in the cart that took him back to town.

Phineas Gage knew what he was doing, and had worked with explosives before that September day in 1858. The young construction foreman was leading a team of workers, using blasting powder to level a piece of land for an upcoming stretch of the Vermont railroad. The process had a rhythm to it: bore a nice deep hole into the rock, fill it with blasting powder and a fuse, then finally pack the powder down with an iron rod before lighting the fuse (and, of course, getting far away).

But something had gone wrong this time. Someone called to Phineas as he was tamping down a charge of powder, and he turned to answer them. His tamping iron sparked against the rock, igniting the blasting powder and sending the more than three-foot-long, inch-wide rod straight through his head. It was astonishing that he didn't die on the spot.

When a doctor came to see the wounded man about half an hour after the accident, Phineas said, "Here is business enough for you, doctor." A massive understatement.

A second doctor, John Martyn Harlow, cleaned the wound and patched it to the best of his ability. Harlow wrote that Gage, still in remarkable possession of his senses, claimed that "he shall be

Phineas Gage holding the tamping iron that injured him

Dr. Harlow

at work in a day or two." That didn't last long. Gage became delirious, then barely conscious. But Dr. Harlow didn't give up. He treated Gage for brain fungus and continued to watch over him. Four weeks after the accident, Gage was awake, with important brain functions intact, like memory and keeping track of time. Another month after that, Gage told Dr. Harlow he was "feeling better in every respect." Gage eventually recovered enough to return to work and daily life—though not at the railroad—and lived twelve more years after the accident.

The reactions to this incredible story were somewhat predictable. There's no way this actually happened, *right*? Many medical professionals dismissed it as lies. A man surely couldn't have a tamping iron blown straight through his head and then get up and *walk around*. But Phineas Gage did, and his one-of-a-kind survival made him a long-lasting legend in medical history.

After his famous patient's death, Harlow published claims that Gage's personality changed massively once he recovered. Gage was known to be a respected and personable foreman with a shrewd, smart mind. But Harlow claimed that Gage became impatient, rude, and incredibly impulsive in his day-to-day life, and that he was unreliable and disrespectful to his coworkers. Harlow said that Gage had trouble holding down jobs after his accident, and depicted him as drifting aimlessly for the remainder of his life.

Later authors took these claims and exaggerated them even further: they depicted Gage as abusive, a bully, a liar, and a drunk. In fact, there is little to no evidence of these behaviors; no one else who knew Gage described him that way. Instead, they remembered the playful adventure stories he told his nieces and nephews, his affection for animals, and the way he pursued recovery and work despite the judgment and rejection he faced from employers because of his injury. Gage did not drift from place to place: he worked at a stable and drove a stagecoach—two skilled, demanding jobs—and did so until his health began to deteriorate.

So why did Harlow depict Gage as a man who had lost his goodness? Most likely because Harlow believed in phrenology, a debunked pseudoscience that claimed complex mental attributes could be traced to small, specific areas (or "organs") of the brain. Phrenology was already widely discredited in Harlow's own time, but his lingering belief may have biased his perception. The "logic" was that humanity's most noble attributes, such as benevolence, would be contained in the top front organ—the exact part of Gage's brain that was injured by the flying tamping iron. So, of *course* he had regressed into a horrible, abusive, rude, no-good man! After all, his organ of benevolence had been nearly obliterated!

Traumatic brain injuries can indeed come with personality changes (just not for the reasons Harlow thought), and the case went on to inspire more research in the still relatively new field of neurology. Harlow's already dubious picture of a man so transformed by his injury that he was "no longer Gage" created a myth that modern scientists have had a hard time shaking. Still, there's no doubt Gage's survival was an incredible feat for both doctor and patient. And Gage surely wasn't completely the same after being impaled through the head by a spike. If you made a miracle recovery and people went around saying it made you a jerk, wouldn't you get a bit cranky too?

FRAUD OF THE CENTURY: THE PILTDOWN MAN

In 1912, Charles Dawson stood before the Geological Society of London and announced that he'd found "the missing link" between humans and apes. At the Piltdown Gravel Pit, he and paleontologist Arthur Smith Woodward had unearthed an ancient skull with both humanlike and apelike features. Their dig also turned up prehistoric stone tools and animal fossils, including an elephant bone.

The skull they discovered, nicknamed "Piltdown Man," would shape the study of human evolution for years to come. Piltdown Man's human-sized brain cavity and apelike jaw illuminated how—and when—ancestral humans might have diverged from their forebears.

It was an incredible discovery. There was just one problem: Dawson faked the whole thing. And he didn't even do a very good job.

Some scientists harbored suspicions from the start, but the hoax persisted until *Time* magazine ran an exposé in 1953. Dawson had combined a medieval human skull, an orangutan's jaw, and fossil teeth from a chimpanzee. He'd "aged" the resulting mashup by staining it with acid—a bit like dipping paper in tea to "antique" it. How did this comically inept craft project fool science for decades? Theories differ, but Piltdown Man appealed to western scientists' biases at the time. They liked the idea of ancient humans first emerging in England; it fit with their grandiose ideas of themselves and their heritage. The skull was even referred to as "The Earliest Englishman." Later investigations revealed that Dawson made a whole career out of tinkering with old bones to create "discoveries." But he and his weird little skeletal sculpture couldn't have achieved much without a parade of yes-men refusing to look too closely at their early Englishman.

Reconstruction of the "Piltdown Man"

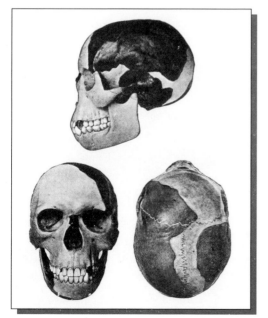

Three views of the "Piltdown Man"

Discover more suspicious skeletons on page 126.

LAWNCHAIR LARRY

If you were alive in 1982 and living in San Pedro, California, you might have seen a colorful assortment of balloons floating across the sky. But whatever, right? You've been to birthday parties. You've seen clowns. But if you had a pair of binoculars on you, you might have felt a chill run down your spine. Because attached to those balloons was a lawn chair. And sitting in that lawn chair was a human man.

Larry Walters, now remembered as Lawnchair Larry, flew spectacularly in the *Inspiration*, his homemade aerostat—a floating aircraft like a blimp—traveling through California skies for forty-five minutes. This was quite the feat, considering that he only expected to get about 100 feet (30 m) high and instead shot up to 16,000 feet (4,900 m)—high enough to be spotted by pilots. The *Inspiration* promptly lived up to its name.

All it takes is a dream, forty-three weather balloons—they're stronger than party balloons, and usually require some sort of permit to launch, which Walters straight-up lied to acquire—a lawn chair, a pellet gun, a radio, and lunch. Oh, and several gallons of water in milk jugs—but we'll get to that later.

And dream Larry did. He couldn't be a pilot due to his poor eyesight, but he figured out the next best thing. At the end of his flight, Lawnchair Larry used his pellet gun to shoot down several balloons and begin his descent. But unfortunately, he didn't think to attach any balloons to his gun, which promptly fell out of his hand and plummeted very fast to the ground.

So on Larry drifted, sinking slowly (after throwing his milk jugs of water overboard to achieve the optimal drift), getting closer to our green beautiful Earth, which might just be how astronauts felt when they saw our little planet from space. At least, that's how they might have felt if they were in lawn chairs. (Unfortunately, NASA didn't think to include those in the Apollo program.) That delicate drift continued until Larry got stuck in a group of power cables, immediately causing a blackout in the neighborhood.

After Larry landed, he was promptly arrested for breaking the law, though how he broke the law and how he would be punished for it wasn't clear. "We know he broke some part of the Federal Aviation Act, and as soon as we decide which part it is, some type of charge will be filed," his confused arresting officer said. "If he had a pilot's license, we'd suspend that, but he doesn't."

Not actually Larry, just another brave balloon-flyer

Larry eventually paid a $1,500 penalty for his sky crimes. And did he regret it? Definitely not. "It was something I had to do," he told reporters after his descent. "I had this dream for twenty years."

If you ever want to get close to this piece of history, you can visit Larry's lawn chair at the Smithsonian. But you'll have to imagine the big blue sky.

THE GREAT STINK

Take a moment to imagine the following nightmare: someone has a really bad butt blast in a shared bathroom, and the smell lingers for months. Now, take that to its extreme, and you've got the entirety of London in the summer of 1858.

When a sewage system is working correctly, most people go around taking it for granted. Public services that impact our quality of life only tend to get noticed when things are, well, crappy. And the sewage system was *not* working in London during the Victorian era. The River Thames, which flows directly through the city, was overflowing with industrial and human waste.

The smell was so putrid that the government spent fortunes pouring chalk lime and carbolic acid into the water to help ease the stench. Aside from not really working, this desperate measure also did nothing to solve the other issue the waste was causing—cholera outbreaks.

Cholera is a nasty and often deadly bacteria. When Britain experienced its first epidemic in 1832, over 50,000 people died. Then in 1848, it happened again, with a similar toll, and a third outbreak hit in 1854. Cholera is typically spread via water, so you probably can guess where this is going. But at the time of the Great Stink, the link between water and cholera wasn't yet a no-brainer.

At the time, most people accepted an ancient theory that contagious diseases were spread by miasma—that people got sick by inhaling "bad air." The idea that fog can poison you with bad vibes ranks lower than germ theory, since it's factually untrue, but ranks significantly higher than "act of God," because the miasma theory encouraged people to build well-ventilated buildings and clean up waste, which both serve to decrease the spread of disease.

So what's a government to do? Well, thanks to the work of one Dr. John Snow, who had traced the worst of a previous cholera outbreak to a polluted water pump, officials knew where to begin. They hired Joseph Bazalgette, a civil engineer and, apparently, sewage genius. He added 82 miles (132 km) of underground sewers and a whopping 1,100 miles (1,800 km) of street sewers, plus new pumping and drainage systems, to keep waste away from the Thames. The final cost: a mere 6.5 million pounds (about $8 million)—worth very close to a billion pounds ($1.2 billion) today.

Totally worth it. If there were any doubts that London needed new sewers (as if a smell so bad it held up Parliament wasn't enough), 1866 brought solid proof. One year after parts of the new sewage system opened, a fourth and final cholera outbreak hit London. This time, the epidemic overwhelmingly affected neighborhoods not yet connected to Bazalgette's new sewage system. The project was completed in 1875, and London was saved from both sickness and stink. At least, they were saved from garbage pileup in the River Thames. Anyone who shares a bathroom knows that you can never truly be free from stink.

Death on the Thames--a totally optimistic depiction of the event from Punch *Magazine*

SANDWICH, M'LORD?
There's no sand in it, so what's the deal?

Humans have been eating bread forever. Or at least, we've been baking a whole lot of it for about ten thousand years. There's some evidence that suggests bread has been around even longer—that people started grinding wild wheat for bread a whole four thousand years before anyone said, "You know what? This would be a lot easier if we had agriculture."

But using bread to carry other food? That's a little more complicated. Back in the first century BCE, the rabbi Hillel the Elder put parts of the Passover meal—bitter herbs and lamb—between two pieces of matzo. In the Middle Ages, peasants often ate their food on "trenchers," blocks of thick, stale bread that served as plates.

By the sixteenth century, you'd see characters in novels and Shakespeare plays shouting about "bread and cheese" and "bread and meat." In his essay "Bread and Meat, for God's Sake," Mark Morton notes that, curiously, the order is never reversed—that is, characters aren't asking for "cheese and bread"—which suggests that people back in Queen Elizabeth I's day already knew and loved a specific food combination that probably looked a lot like a sandwich.

However, the word "sandwich" in the modern sense wasn't recorded until about two centuries later, in 1762. And its legendary namesake was John Montagu, the Fourth Earl of Sandwich. (Sandwich, by the way, was an important port in England. That's why he was called that.)

As the story goes, Montagu loved to play cards and would sit in one spot and gamble for hours on end, so it's probably for the best that he was alive long before the invention of video games. Late one night, he asked his servant to bring him something easy to eat that would not make a mess. What he got was a nice hunk of salted meat between two slices of bread. It was not only an energizing meal, but it also kept him from getting grease on his fingers (or his cards).

I'm John Montagu, Fourth Earl of Sandwich

In the earl's defense, he wasn't just a gambler—he had a busy government job, and his new favorite meal could have also helped him not spill meat grease on important Cabinet documents. But what's a more fun thing to name a food after: something you eat at your desk, or something you eat at an old-timey table while you're kicking people's butts at cards?

Popularity skyrocketed. People all over the country began to order "the same as Sandwich," and eventually, they were eaten all over the world.

Current Earl of Sandwich, John Edward Hollister Montagu

Can you see the resemblance?

The current Earl of Sandwich—yes, there still is one— thinks this is pretty great. Continuing his family's legacy, he invested in a chain of sandwich shops that operates in several countries (oddly not including England). We can't speak to his card game, though.

For more breakthroughs in sandwich technology, see page 19!

DEATH BY VOTER FRAUD

On October 3, 1849, at Ryan's Tavern in Baltimore, Maryland, a man was discovered in a state of "beastly intoxication." His hair was dirty and bedraggled, his face unwashed, and his clothes were grimy, worn, and didn't fit him at all. He was incoherent and delirious. His gaze was said to be "lusterless and vacant." They could get almost no information out of the man—other than vague snatches of conversation with "spectral and imaginary objects on the walls." He was sent to the hospital, and died several days later of uncertain causes.

This disheveled, unintelligible man was none other than the author Edgar Allan Poe. A major literary figure in his own time, his stories of mystery and the macabre remain widely read and influential today. His story "The Murders in the Rue Morgue" has been described as the first modern detective story, and many of his works contributed to the still-budding genre of science fiction. His poem "The Raven" became one of the most famous works of poetry ever penned.

But that's enough accolades—let's get back to Baltimore. How exactly did Poe come to be in that tavern? The circumstances surrounding his death are certainly peculiar. Poe was dressed in clothes that were entirely out of character for him, both in style and in general shabbiness—most people described him as a handsome man who kept his stylish black frockcoats and cravats well mended. His whereabouts were also entirely unknown for several days leading up to the event. Some believe it was murder or suicide. Others blame rabies, syphilis, or cholera. But perhaps the most interesting theory claims that Poe was a victim of *cooping*, a form of electoral fraud.

Cooping involved kidnapping citizens off the street and forcing them to vote a certain way in a local election. Victims were threatened with violence—and sometimes subjected to it—and given substantial amounts of alcohol to make them easier to influence. They were then commonly made to vote not just once, but multiple times. To accomplish this, their captors would dress them in an array of different outfits, sometimes even in wigs and fake beards. They would then send them to the polls as many times as they could, hoping to rig the election through the extra votes.

Was Poe a victim of cooping? Though the strange clothes and drunkenness seem to suggest it, there's no way to know for sure. His untimely demise remains shrouded in mystery, like a raven repeating again and again, "Nevermore," while you're trying to sleep.

THE ULTIMATE COMPUTER BUG

Usually, when someone says that their computer has a bug, they just mean that it isn't working right, not that some insect is working its way into the circuitry like a worm burrowing into an apple.

But in 1947, that's exactly what happened. Engineers at Harvard University, while working on the Mark II computer—a 25-ton megamachine commissioned by the U.S. Navy, nothing like the small, portable devices we use today—discovered something stuck in one of the components. It wasn't a trick of the eye. There was actually a bug in the computer—a small moth.

The group extracted the insect, taped it to the logbook, and then proudly labeled it "first actual case of bug being found." In 1947, this was funny, and it still is, but now it's also a historical artifact. The logbook (and the poor moth) is on display at the Smithsonian's National Museum of American History.

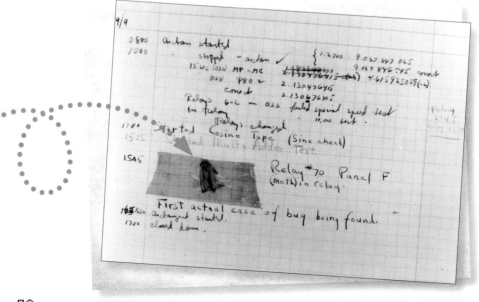

The moth incident may have helped spread the term "debugging" outside the computer programming world, but engineers and inventors had already been calling machine problems "bugs" for a long time. By the time the first electric computer was invented, "bug" was already in the dictionary as "a defect in an apparatus or its operation." And Thomas Edison had already dealt with such difficulties forty-five years before that. In 1889, the *Pall Mall Gazette* wrote that Edison "had been up the two previous nights discovering a 'bug' in his phonograph." It's fun to wonder if he found any bugs while creating the first ever cat video—you know, the one from page 24?

The Ultimate Computer/ Footstool/Toilet

As computers spread from military complexes to college campuses to family homes, there were still some "bugs" to work out—at least in terms of what the computers were *supposed* to do. In 1999, you could buy an Intel Ottoman PC, a computer that could not only browse the web and play movies, but also served as a functional footrest. Simply close the computer, put your feet on the padded cushion, and relax! Unfortunately, this invention did not catch on—it's very easy to break a computer you're supposed to put your feet on, and some people noticed it looked a little too much like a toilet. But the nineties were a decade still remembered for its dreamers.

MIKE THE HEADLESS CHICKEN

Sometimes executions don't go quite as planned. For that matter, neither does dinner.

On September 10, 1945, a farmer named Lloyd Olsen went out to process some chickens for market. One of these birds was a small Wyandotte chicken named Mike. Lloyd would kill the chickens, and his wife Clara would clean them.

However, when the deed was done, and Mike's head was no longer attached to his body, he surprised the whole family by remaining, well, *alive*. Chickens are known to stagger for a bit after the deed is done, but even the next morning, Mike seemed completely fine. He walked around the yard like nothing had happened. How could it be?

The Olsens took Mike to the University of Utah in Salt Lake City to find out. It turned out that although the axe removed most of his head, it had missed Mike's jugular vein and left most of his brain stem intact. Because a lot of a chicken's brain is in the back of its head, Mike could still breathe, walk, digest food, and balance on a perch—all classic chicken activities.

Given that Mike survived his first beheading, the Olsen family decided to spare him a second one and take care of him. They fed Mike corn, worms, and water through an eyedropper, and removed mucus from his throat via syringe. Neighbors from all over town came to see if the incredible story of Mike was true. Soon, word spread beyond the neighborhood—Mike was a sensation. So the

Olsens decided there was only one thing to do: take the show on the road.

The miracle chicken appeared in papers all over the country, and was even featured in *Time* magazine. For eighteen months, the Olsens showed Mike off at fairs, carnivals, and sideshows. Members of the public could view him for twenty-five cents, and at the peak of his popularity, Mike could draw up to six hundred visitors a day! That's $150 every day, which today is equal to more than $2,000. Mike toured Long Beach, California, as well as Arizona and parts of the southeast USA.

But, like so many celebrities after him, tragedy cut Mike's life of stardom short. One spring day, Mike suddenly disappeared. When people asked what happened, Lloyd simply said that he sold Mike for a profit, and would say no more about it.

It wasn't until the 1980s that the sad truth was revealed. On March 17, 1947, while on tour in Arizona, the Olsens discovered Mike choking on mucus. The family looked for the syringe but realized that they had accidentally left it at a previous touring spot. There was nothing they could do.

While Mike passed away, his memory lives on. The city of Fruita, Colorado, celebrates Mike the Headless Chicken Festival every year on the first weekend of June. Visitors can celebrate Mike by viewing exotic poultry from around the country, listening to live music, and participating in a wing-eating contest.

Rock on, Mike!

THE BUTTERED CAT PARADOX

Some words of wisdom have been taught for ages, passed down from generation to generation, like "better late than never," and "the five-second rule" (the glue that holds society together).

But what happens when two of those adages contradict each other? Consider the following sayings:

> Cats always land on their feet.
> Buttered toast will always land buttered side down.

So what would happen if you attached a piece of buttered toast to a cat and then pushed it out of a tree? Would the cat land on its feet? Or would the force of the buttered toast prevail and leave the cat flat on its back?

The original theory was submitted by John Frazee for a contest in *OMNI* magazine, a publication interested in paradoxes—statements that logically can't be true. Frazee won a prize for his paradox, and the idea took off from there, explored in movies, comics, and late-night TV. A cat unable to land on its back, tied to a piece of toast unable to land right-side-up, floating forever in midair—what a mental image. Tragic, compelling, and a little hilarious.

Okay, but what *would* happen? Unfortunately, the answer isn't too exciting. Cats would still land on their feet. The mechanism behind this is called the "cat righting reflex"—basically, cats have a very flexible backbone and a free-floating collarbone, so they can twist superfast in midair when falling.

In case you didn't already know, toast is an inanimate object, and it's not particularly heavy, so it doesn't have the power required to bring cats to their knees (well, backs, in this case). However, if you're curious why buttered toast almost always falls buttered side down, there are some interesting physics at play.

It's not just bad luck. It has to do with the position the toast starts at: in your hands, buttered side up. When it falls to the ground, there's only enough time for the toast to rotate about half a turn. So if all humans were ten feet tall, then the age-old saying might be "buttered toast will always land buttered side up." But then there'd be no paradox, and no floating cat cartoons. Also we wouldn't fit through most doors.

THE CASE OF THE COTTINGLEY FAIRIES

Sherlock Holmes: the world's most famous fictional detective. For way more than a century, stories starring Sherlock have demonstrated the importance of deductive reasoning, of questioning and looking past a simple first impression. So if someone came to you with photographs of magical creatures—Bigfoot, the Loch Ness Monster, dragon eggs, whatever—and you were a fan of Sherlock Holmes, you would take these sightings with a grain of salt, right? Right.

It stands to reason that Sir Arthur Conan Doyle, the author of *Sherlock Holmes*, would be a fan of Sherlock Holmes. So one might assume he would be similarly discerning. But no matter how clever you think you are, there could always be someone out there who's a greater mastermind than you.

Conan Doyle's not-so-great real-life detective story begins in the summer of 1917, when two young girls, cousins Frances Griffiths and Elsie Wright, set out to prove that fairies were real. At least, they set out to make their families *believe* that fairies were real. They borrowed Elsie's father's camera and went into the forest to take photos of the magical creatures up close. When they returned, it was with cold, hard, proof. Or something that looked like proof, anyway.

To their family they showed two pictures: one of Frances surrounded by four sprites,

dancing playfully while a waterfall tumbled in the distance, and one of Elsie shaking hands with a friendly gnome in a patch of grass. The family wasn't fully convinced—that is, they didn't necessarily believe that the fairies in the photographs were real, but if the images were faked, they didn't know how the trick was done. And the girls certainly wouldn't say.

A few years later, Elsie's mother took the photographs to England's branch of the Theosophical Society, a spiritual movement that pulled from occult and magical beliefs from around the world. The pictures caught the attention of a leading Theosophist, Edward Gardner, who was beyond excited to have proof that magic was real. Not that he needed proof. He knew magic was real. Totally.

A photography expert took a look at the photos and promised they were totally, absolutely for real. Satisfied, Gardner gave a series of lectures on the photos in 1920—with copies for sale at a profit, of course.

And then they came to Arthur Conan Doyle. In addition to writing detective novels, he was also working on a magazine article about fairies and spiritualism. The idea of a world beyond the edges of our own enchanted him. He wrote that the potential existence of fairies would force the world to "admit that there is a glamour and a mystery to life," adding, "I look on the prospect with awe."

The interest of such a famous author was a big deal for the fairies-are-real movement. But Conan Doyle, with his Holmesian curiosity, said he needed more proof to be fully convinced.

Challenge accepted. The following year, Elsie and Frances produced two new photos, each with a girl and fairy facing one another in idyllic woodland scenes. After pondering the evidence, including studying the photos through an actual high-end magnifying glass, Conan Doyle was sold.

Fairies Photographed

AN
EPOCH-MAKING EVENT
.... DESCRIBED BY

A. CONAN DOYLE

SHOULD the incidents here narrated, and the photographs attached, hold their own against the criticism which they will excite, it is no exaggeration to say that they will mark an epoch in human thought. I put them and all the evidence before the public for examination and judgment. If I am myself asked whether I consider the case to be absolutely and finally proved, I should answer that in order to remove the last faint shadow of doubt I should wish to see the result repeated before a disinterested witness. At the same time, I recognize the difficulty of such a request, since rare results must be obtained when and how they can. But short of final and absolute proof, I consider, after carefully going into every possible source of error, that a strong *prima facie* case has been built up. The cry of " fake " is sure to be raised, and will make some impression upon those who have not had the opportunity of knowing the people concerned, or the place. On the photographic side every objection has been considered and adequately met. The pictures stand or fall together. Both are false, or both are true. All the circumstances point to the latter alternative, and yet in a matter involving so tremendous a new departure one needs overpowering evidence before one can say that there is no conceivable loophole for error.

It was about the month of May in this year that I received a letter from Miss Felicia Scatcherd, so well known in several departments of human thought, to the effect that two photographs of fairies had been taken in the North of England under circumstances which seemed to put fraud out of the question. The statement would have appealed to me at any time, but I happened at the moment to be collecting material for an article on fairies, now completed, and I had accumulated a surprising number of cases of people who claimed to be able to see these little creatures. The evidence was so complete and detailed, with such good names attached to it, that it was difficult to believe that it was false; but, being by nature of a somewhat sceptical turn, I felt that something closer was needed before I could feel personal conviction and assure myself that these were not thought-forms conjured up by the imagination or expectation of the seers. The rumour of the photographs interested me deeply, therefore, and following the matter up from one lady informant to another, I came at last upon Mr. Edward L. Gardner, who has been ever since my most efficient collaborator, to whom all credit is due. Mr. Gardner, it may be remarked, is a member of the Executive Committee of the Theosophical Society, and a well-known lecturer upon occult subjects.

He had not himself at that time mastered the whole case, but all he had he placed freely at my disposal. I had already seen prints of the photographs, but I was relieved to find that he had the actual negatives, and that it was from them, and not from the prints, that two expert photographers, especially Mr. Snelling, of 26, The Bridge, Wealdstone, Harrow, had already formed their conclusions in favour of the genuineness of the pictures. Mr. Gardner tells his own story presently, so I will simply say that at that period he had got into direct and friendly touch with the Carpenter family. We are compelled to use a pseudonym and to with-

Vol. lx.—31

In his next article, he argued that the fact that it was children, not adults, who often reported seeing fairies throughout history, was evidence of their existence. He used his own family as an example:

> "My younger family consists of two little boys and one small girl, very truthful children, each of whom tells with detail the exact circumstances and appearance of the creature. To each it happened only once, and in each case it was a single little figure, twice in the garden, once in the nursery. Inquiry among friends shows that many children have had the same experience, but they close up at once when met by ridicule and incredulity."

In other words, if adults took children seriously, Conan Doyle believed that even more would admit to seeing these magical creatures, and more proof of their existence would appear.

Conan Doyle did not live long enough to further explore this phenomenon. For sixty years, the story behind the photographs remained a mystery beyond the reach of even Sherlock Holmes. But in 1983, the world finally learned the truth about the images: Frances and Elsie confessed they were fakes. Inspired by illustrations in *Princess Mary's Gift Book*, a popular picture book from their childhood, the girls drew dancers with wings to design their own fairies. Then, they cut out their drawings and secured them to the real-life trees and flowers using hatpins.

(Speaking of hatpins—did you hear about the twentieth-century hatpin panic? No? Check out page 74.)

Elsie and Frances had truly outsmarted the master of mystery. Conan Doyle actually had deduced that Elsie may have drawn the fairies—he'd heard she was an artist, and was naturally suspicious. But her drawing skills had been put to the test—by Edward Gardner (again, the guy who made a living by claiming these photos were real; how's that for suspicious?)—who reported that the beautiful, realistic creatures from the pictures were far beyond Elsie's artistic abilities. Plus, everyone who knew the girls described them as open and honest—too innocent to stick to such a lie.

Ultimately, the work of these devious masterminds was really just a prank that got away from them. "I never even thought of it being a fraud," admitted an elderly Frances, who was only nine when she'd taken the pictures. "It was just Elsie and I having a bit of fun. . . . People often say to me, 'Don't you feel ashamed that you have made all these poor people look like fools? They believed in you.' But I do not, because they wanted to believe."

Arthur Conan Doyle sure did. While he wrote stories about sniffing out the truth, he hoped at the same time that humanity would find out the real world was stranger than fiction. For him, and countless others, the Cottingley Fairies helped strengthen that hope. And before you laugh, consider: if the story were special enough, don't you think you'd believe in it too?

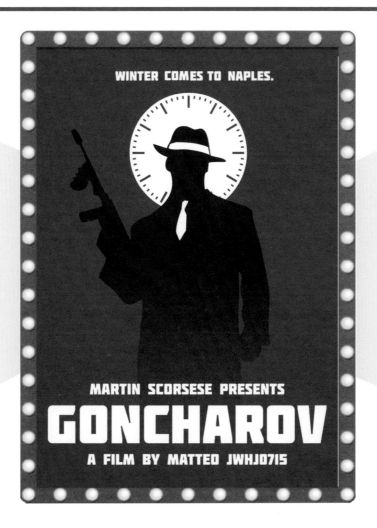

WINTER COMES TO NAPLES.

MARTIN SCORSESE PRESENTS

GONCHAROV

A FILM BY MATTEO JWHJ0715

GONCHAROV (1973) (2022)

Have you seen *Goncharov*? It has all the hallmarks of a masterpiece. The premise itself is captivating: Goncharov, a Russian mafia boss, has set up shop in Naples after the fall of the Soviet Union. His marriage to Katya is growing strained, and he struggles with the budding romantic entanglement between him and his greatest rival (Andrei "The Banker"), even as Andrei tries to tear down his criminal empire.

The bridge scene has the tension of a steel cable about to snap. The recurring motif of clocks is both poignant and bitterly tragic. John Cazale as "Ice Pick Joe" is a grim reminder of the far-reaching consequences of violence.

Goncharov is bloody, witty, and visually breathtaking. It's a beautiful movie.

It also doesn't exist, and never has.

"Goncharov" is an internet meme that grew to staggering proportions. It started with a pair of knockoff boots with a strange label that read:

The greatest mafia move ever made
MARTIN SCORSESE presents
GONCHAROV
a DOMENICO PROCACCI production
a film by matteo jwhj0715
about the naples mafia

An unlucky (or very lucky) shopper got these boots online and shared a picture of the "apparently nonexistent Martin Scorsese movie???" on the label.

Another user replied, "this idiot hasn't seen *Goncharov*."

After that, things got weirder.

The internet came together to make this "apparently nonexistent" movie a forgotten classic from 1973. An artist named Alex Korotchuk created a movie poster for *Goncharov* featuring mob-movie legends such as Robert De Niro and Harvey Keitel. Inspired by the art, and charmed by the boots' cryptic text, people got swept away talking about various scenes in the movie, discussing the themes that it dealt with, and ranking their favorite characters and performances. They shipped characters, created music, and wrote reviews and critical essays about the film and its plot.

Every last bit was made up, and what resulted was the idea of a movie, molded by the collective imagination of everyone who contributed to it.

In this process, certain elements of *Goncharov* have been generally agreed on. It has a star-studded cast that includes Robert De Niro, Cybill Shepherd, Al Pacino, Gene Hackman, and Harvey Keitel. Martin Scorsese was either the director or a producer. It was released in 1973 after a long and troubled production. It was forgotten for a number of years and became extremely difficult to find. Goncharov's underling Mario betrays him at some point. And, after betrayal upon betrayal, Goncharov dies at the end.

With some detective work, a user traced the probable origin of the text on the boot—a machine-garbled version of the poster for a very grim, real-life mafia movie "presented by" Martin Scorsese for a film festival. (Not that that explains why it was printed on a boot.) But the made-up *Goncharov* kept its hold on the imagination—even though the identity of Matteo JWHJ0715 remains shrouded in mystique. Some fans have gone so far as to make cinematic trailers for the movie. There are nearly one thousand *Goncharov* fanfiction works. And a few weeks after its creation, copies of Korotchuk's poster were pasted on the streets of New York City, alongside promotions for real movies and shows. It may only be a matter of time before a particularly eager fan picks up a camera and decides to make *Goncharov* a reality. Anyone know what Scorsese is up to these days?

THE BLUE FUGATES OF TROUBLESOME CREEK

The sight of Benjamin "Benjy" Stacy shocked doctors as well as his parents. In almost all respects, he looked like a perfectly healthy baby. There was just one key difference: he was entirely blue. Alarmed, the doctors rushed him to the University of Kentucky Medical Center for blood tests. Nothing turned up; the hospital was stumped. But Benjy's grandmother held the key to this medical mystery, and it was the story of their family. It was the tale of the Blue Fugates of Troublesome Creek.

Over 150 years before Benjy's strange birth, a man named Martin Fugate and his wife Elizabeth Smith claimed land in Kentucky along the banks of Troublesome Creek. Martin Fugate had traveled to the United States from France, gotten married, settled down—a regular man with a regular story, except for one thing: his skin was blue.

The couple had seven children together, four of them carrying Martin's blue tint. For generations afterward, the Fugates (and later the Smiths, Stacys, and Ritchies) continued to be born from time to time with the same blue skin.

For well over a hundred years, no one knew what caused this. If it was a disorder or disease, it didn't seem to be making them sick. Descendants of Martin and Elizabeth often lived well into their eighties and nineties, blue-skinned or not. Many of their neighbors found it strange; some suspected the work of the devil.

It wasn't until the second half of the twentieth century, when the blood doctor Madison Cawein arrived on the scene, that the mystery unraveled. He first heard about blue people in 1960 while working

in Lexington, Kentucky. Intrigued, he journeyed to the hills of Hazard, near Troublesome Creek, to see if the rumors were true.

He heard stories: one from a nurse, Ruth Pendergrass, about a woman who came inside from the cold and asked for a blood test. Her skin was so blue, almost deep purple, that Pendergrass thought the woman might drop dead on the spot. But the woman wasn't worried. She was a Fugate, after all.

Cawein and Pendergrass searched over hills and hollows, catching glimpses of blue faces in the distance which then disappeared without a trace. This continued for months until Cawein grew frustrated, and he was on the verge of giving up. Just when he'd almost stopped hoping for answers, Patrick and Rachel Ritchie walked into the clinic where he worked.

They were, undeniably, blue.

Cawein examined them. The siblings weren't sick, at least not according to any tests he ordered. In the absence of danger, the three began mapping the lineage of their blue family, all the way back to Martin Fugate.

Cawein had an idea where the blue was coming from, and it had something to do with the makeup of the family's blood. He suspected that they had *methemoglobinemia*—too much methemoglobin in their blood. Methemoglobin is a form of hemoglobin, the protein in red blood cells that helps move oxygen throughout the body. But methemoglobin cannot bond with oxygen, which means two things: it can't help a red blood cell do its most important job, and, incidentally, it happens to look blue.

Most people's blood has less than 1 percent methemoglobin. Having more than 20 percent can lead to some pretty serious health issues, since, famously, we need oxygen to live. But having, say, 5 to 10 percent methemoglobin in your blood probably won't cause any problems. It might, however, turn your skin a very deep blue shade.

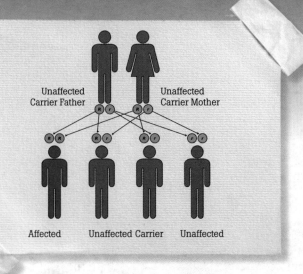

*Parents can pass on a gene to their children
even if they don't display the trait themselves.*

Cawein tested the Ritchies' blood, and blood from other members of their family. And the tests proved that he was right. They were missing an enzyme (a protein that causes chemical reactions) called diaphorase, which converts blue methemoglobin back to good old oxygen-carrying hemoglobin.

The treatment was simple: Cawein gave the siblings a solution of methylene—which is, ironically, blue—that reduced the methemoglobin. Just minutes after the injection, the blue tint faded, and the Ritchies' faces flushed a soft pink.

Because the medicine's effect is only temporary, the doctor gave all the blue family members a supply of methylene blue pills. Taking them every day kept the blue tint away and the oxygen flowing freely, in exchange for the minor side effect of blue pee.

Martin Fugate's methemoglobin problem gene had weakened by the time it got to his great-great-great-great-grandson Benjy Stacy in 1975, so Benjy wasn't blue for long. As he grew older, the blue would appear only in Benjy's fingernails and lips when he got cold, the final tinges of blue in his family.

HOW (NOT) TO ACHIEVE IMMORTALITY

Do you want to live forever? You're not alone. Throughout history, people have searched for the secret to eternal life. Today, they might try blood transfusions and specific off-hours sleep schedules, or plasma facials and cellular rejuvenation, but even in the distant past, the desire to escape one's mortal coil drove human beings to the far edges of this earth.

The first emperor of China, Qin Shi Huang, was one such person. He sent ships full of soldiers, sailors, sorcerers, and servants overseas to acquire potions that would grant him eternal life. Believing that mercury could sustain him, he often drank mercury-laced wine sweetened with honey. He died at the age of 49, most likely due to mercury poisoning, and was buried in a mausoleum as large as an entire city. Eight thousand life-size terracotta warriors were built to guard the vast underground tomb where Qin Shi Huang would rest for all time. Although he may have fallen short of immortality, decorating his grave with world wonders was a solid option B.

The emperor was not the only one who believed poisonous metals had anti-aging properties. Diane de Poitiers, the mistress of King Henry II of France, drank an elixir of gold chloride, mercury, and ether every day to keep her youthful appearance. This luxurious,

amazingly unsafe elixir made her hair extremely fine, and her skin as white as porcelain. By extension, she also had extremely fragile bones, skin, and teeth. In 2008, when scientists unearthed her body, they discovered five hundred times above the normal level of gold in locks of her hair (did you know there's such a thing as a normal level of gold in your hair?), as well as a healthy dose of mercury. (And by healthy we mean really, really unhealthy. Like, twice-as-much-as-you-can-have-before-it-kills-you unhealthy.) She died at age 66, which, as you may notice, is nowhere near living forever. But a lord who knew her wrote that she was still as "fresh and also pleasant as she had been at thirty years of age" by the time she kicked the bucket, so hey, maybe she thought it was worth it.

Some of humanity's oldest and most important stories have explored the theme of immortality and what we might risk to seek it. Gilgamesh, a half-god king from a four-thousand-year-old poem, tyrannized ancient Mesopotamia until the gods sent a man named Enkidu to be his companion. When Enkidu died, Gilgamesh was in anguish. He refused to accept that all his riches couldn't stop death from claiming somebody he loved, or that somebody as powerful as him would one day die too. So he said "no thanks" to mortal limitations, and sought out eternal life.

He met the world's last immortal, who told him he must stay awake for six days. When he failed at that, he went to find a magical life-giving plant at the bottom of the sea. He retrieved it, but a snake ate it out of his hand. The plant was so powerful that snakes forever after shed their skins, revealing new bodies underneath. Humbled, Gilgamesh returned home without Enkidu and without the secret to everlasting life. But their story was written in clay and passed down for thousands of years, and today we can still read about their adventures.

So, in a way, people can live forever—when their names and their stories live on long after they're dead. The ancient Greeks had a word for this type of immortality: *kleos*. Heroes in Greek myths were all about kleos. Having a glorious reputation, famous offspring, or a really long poem about you was way better than literal eternal life. When the Trojan War broke out, the soldier Achilles was offered a choice: survive the war and grow old in obscurity, or come to a violent end that the world would remember forever. Since it's been three thousand years and you know who Achilles is, you can guess what he picked.

If you'd like to hear about a quest for immortality that's not a bummer, there's Sun Wukong, a magic monkey from the four-hundred-year-old Chinese classic *Journey to the West*. He was born from an egg made of stone, became the Monkey King, and decided  he and his subjects should get to live fun monkey lives forever. So he learned to shapeshift, surf on clouds, leap for thousands of miles, make himself amazingly tiny and big, and beat up dragon kings. Eventually he fought his way to heaven and wiped all the monkeys from the Book of Life and Death—immortality, easy as that. Of course, he was later trapped in a rock for half a millennium, poisoned, disemboweled, beheaded, boiled, and burned. But, as befits one of the world's first and favorite superheroes, the Monkey King always bounced back to fight another day.

We hope it's obvious, but please don't try any of this at home. No gold, no mercury, no all-nighters, no deals with gods, no cloud-surfing, and please, *please* no going to the bottom of the sea.

NAPOLEON'S MOST TERRIFYING BATTLE

Napoleon is remembered for many things; some of them true, like declaring himself the emperor of France, and some of them not true, like him being super short—he was dead average height for a French guy at the time.

But sometimes, there are things from history we tend not to remember at all, and for Napoleon, that would include one of his greatest defeats.

In 1807, Napoleon was really on a roll. He had just signed the Treaties of Tilsit, which put an end to the war between the French and Russian empires. And this, he decided, was worth a celebration. Back then, the best way to celebrate peace was to hunt animals for sport, so that's exactly what Napoleon set out to do.

Three thousand rabbits later, the party was ready to begin. But as soon as the cages were opened, those thousands of rabbits did the unthinkable: they didn't flee in terror. In fact, quite the opposite of fleeing in terror, they ran *at* Napoleon and his guests headfirst, sowing fear and chaos in the group.

It didn't help that the rabbits in question were not wild animals, who fear humans as predators, but domesticated bunnies, who expect humans to feed them, pick them up, and take photos of them in silly scenarios. The bunnies swarmed the party, who tried and failed to beat them back with an arsenal ranging from muskets to sticks. Overwhelmed by the rabbits' military strategy, Napoleon surrendered and just barely escaped to his carriage.

Or so he thought. The rabbits, fearless, flanked the party and made their way to Napoleon's coach. Some accounts describe the emperor flinging lingering bunnies out the window as his carriage finally left the scene.

You can overthrow a monarchy, conquer most of Europe, go toe to toe with a mighty opponent and come out on top. But the Battle of the Bunnies just goes to show that you can't win them all.

Napoleon's Alternate Career Path

In addition to being an ambitious military strategist, Napoleon was also an aspiring author. He wrote a romance novel called *Clisson et Eugénie*, which was a thinly veiled fictional retelling of Napoleon's own romance with Eugénie Désirée Clary, the Queen of Sweden. Unfortunately, he was born too early for glowing online reviews or a bestselling book tour, so he had to settle for ruling a huge chunk of Europe instead.

THE HATPIN PERIL

It was the early 1900s, and a strange hysteria was gripping the world. People were up in arms, politicians made impassioned speeches, and city councils passed strict new laws to protect against the danger presented by . . . hatpins.

A hatpin is exactly what it sounds like: a long pin meant for holding a hat in place. Usually 6 to 8 inches (15 to 20 cm) long, with a pinhead that may or may not be decorated, they are pierced through a hat and into the wearer's hair. Longer than your normal pin, certainly, but not much of a deadly weapon.

But you might think twice, had you seen or heard the public backlash against the so-called "hatpin peril." Tabloids described them as "murderous weapons" and "swords." Questionable tales circulated like wildfire: A girl from Scranton jokingly thrust her hatpin at her boyfriend, only to pierce him through the heart. A passenger on a New York City streetcar had his ear jabbed by a lady's hatpin and was dead in a week from infection. Hatpins were even, according to one story, the weapon of choice for an all-female anarchist mob attack.

What was *actually* happening was quite different. Some people were using their hatpins as weapons: this was true. As more women worked and traveled outside the home at the turn of the century, they came into contact with "mashers"—a term for a predator dressed like a gentleman. The original reports of hatpin attacks depicted ordinary women using improvised weapons to protect themselves from men who were attacking or threatening them. Women were wielding their hatpins in self-defense. How *dare* they!

Unable to argue with the desire to be left alone in public—the real reason for the pin-jabbing incidents—some critics worked up a frenzy over the method. Hatpins were clearly dangerous instruments, and women could, and would, injure and even kill innocent men if they remained street legal. A number of cities sprang to action: their councils passed laws that banned hatpins over a certain length, and were celebrated for it by many and protested by others. Chicago, New Orleans, Baltimore, Pittsburgh, Massachusetts, and New Jersey enacted such laws. The trend swept through Australia, too—sixty women were jailed in Sydney after refusing to pay fines for their pins.

Not everyone took the supposed threat so seriously. The laws were often unenforced, with police reluctant to stop random women and demand their hatpin measurements. The "hatpin panic" started to die down at the start of World War I; you might think people realized there were more important things to worry about, but really, large hatpins were falling out of fashion (and possibly harder to produce due to wartime metal shortages). By the 1920s, the type of people who worried women's fashion was a menace to society had moved on to "flappers," who had short hair and knew rude words. In the 1950s, beaches worldwide banned the scandalous bikini. Ironically, around the same time, the American actress Elsa Lanchester came out with a popular version of a funny old song: "Never Go Walking Out Without Your Hat Pin," celebrating a granny's favorite form of self-defense.

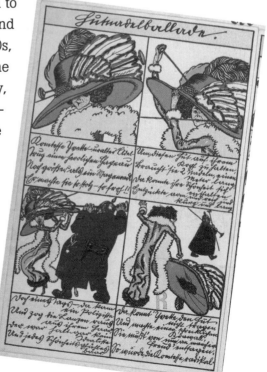

Another unconventional style of self-defense? Bartitsu. What? You never heard of Bartitsu? (Page 102.)

KENTUCKY MEAT SHOWER

Winter was almost over in Olympia Springs, Kentucky. The last snows of the season had passed, and any cold rains that might come would only signal the beginning of spring growths. But on March 3, 1876, outside Allen Crouch's house, it was neither rain nor snow that fell from the sky.

Crouch's wife was making soap when it started. The sky was clear, and then it wasn't. Pieces fell around her like large snowflakes. But pieces of what, exactly? Well, meat. Mystery meat, raining down in chunks bigger than golf balls.

The next day, onlookers saw proof of the storm across the Crouches' football-field-sized patch of land, with pieces of meat sticking to fences and strewn all over the ground. When it fell, Allen Crouch noticed it was fresh. But within the day it began to dry. Two men ate a bit of it (for some reason) and said it tasted like "either mutton or venison."

Scientists examined the meat and found traces of lung and muscle tissue. One of them thought it must be frogspawn; another was sure that it was simply a fleshy-looking fungus. But if it were frogspawn or fungus, why would it have lung tissue? demanded a third. And not only were they desperate to know what the meat was—how in the world did it get into Allen Crouch's yard? And also, why *only* Allen Crouch's yard?

The most convincing theory was simple, if disgusting, and came from the locals themselves. What fell over the Crouches' home was not fungus or alien meat, but bird vomit. Specifically, vulture vomit. In the days before the start of spring, when vultures are full—too full—and flying through the sky, they're known to throw up, either for self-defense or greater air speed. One of these coordinated vomits was carried by a gentle breeze to the Crouches' house. The meat shower sparked scientific inquiry, gained public interest, and ruined at least one batch of soap. Let's just hope those guys who ate it were okay.

FLESH DESCENDING IN A SHOWER.

AN ASTOUNDING PHENOMENON IN KENTUCKY—FRESH MEAT LIKE MUTTON OR VENISON FALLING FROM A CLEAR SKY.

Special Dispatch to the New-York Times.

LOUISVILLE, March 9.—The Bath County (Ky.) News of this date says: "On last Friday a shower of meat fell near the house of Allen Crouch, who lives some two or three miles from the Olympian Springs in the southern portion of the county, covering a strip of ground about one hundred yards in length and fifty wide. Mrs. Crouch was out in the yard at the time, engaged in making soap, when meat which looked like beef began to fall around her. The sky was perfectly clear at the time, and she said it fell like large snow flakes, the pieces as a general thing not being much larger. One piece fell near her which was three or four inches square. Mr. Harrison Gill, whose veracity is unquestionable, and from whom we obtained the above facts, hearing of the occurrence visited the locality the next day, and says he saw particles of meat sticking to the fences and scattered over the ground. The meat when it first fell appeared to be perfectly fresh.

The correspondent of the Louisville Commercial, writing from Mount Sterling, corroborates the above, and says the pieces of flesh were of various sizes and shapes, some of them being two inches square. Two gentlemen, who tasted the meat, express the opinion that it was either mutton or venison.

The New York Times
Published: March 10, 1876
Copyright © The New York Times

FIGHTING TOOTH AND NAIL (AND WHISKER AND TAIL)

For thousands of years, cats have been beloved members of households, friendly faces at street corners, and even revered figures, appearing in religious tombs and monuments across the globe. But this warm, fuzzy relationship took a dark turn during the Middle Ages, when one man declared that cats were ministers of witchcraft.

On June 13, 1233, Pope Gregory IX released his first papal bull—an important religious decree. The bull, called *Vox in Rama*, called on Christians to get busy persecuting witches, and included an alarming account of how witches were initiated into devil worship. First, said the pope, novice witches would meet an extremely large frog. Then a strange pale man would appear, and erase all memories of their faith in the Catholic Church. And finally, the coven (group of witches) would symbolically declare allegiance to a black cat by kissing its butt. After all this was done, they'd get a visit from Lucifer, who was allegedly part cat.

Even though this description is clearly bananas, medieval audiences tended to agree that cats had ties to witchcraft. Many people believed that killing cats could break evil spells; across the continent, cats were beaten, thrown from churches, and even burned. Remnants of this violence remain in certain yearly festivals, although they now throw stuffed cats instead of real ones out the window during *Kattenstoet* in Belgium, and when kids at Denmark's *Fastelavn* hit a candy-filled barrel with sticks piñata-style, there's no longer a live cat inside.

A century after *Vox in Rama*, the Black Death, a brutal outbreak

of bubonic plague primarily carried by rats, ravaged the Eurasian continent. Closer to our own time, a myth arose that Pope Gregory's declaration was partly responsible. If only there had been more cats in Europe, the theory goes, perhaps the plague wouldn't have spread so far.

But while it's fun to think that cats can save the world—and hey, maybe they can—this really isn't true. For one, the plague wasn't spread by rats directly, but by the fleas they carried, which could jump to other animals, including cats. More cats could very well have meant more plague, not less. Plus, Europe had plenty of terriers, which were and still are great at hunting rats, and they were neither accused of witchcraft nor super effective at stopping the plague.

Besides, although medieval Europe may not have been the most fun time or place to be a feline, *Vox in Rama* and witchcraft panic didn't actually do anything to wipe out cats. Gregory may have been, well let's say *concerned*, about Satanic rituals, but he didn't go so far as to tell anyone to kill their cats, and even when people did kill cats, it wasn't in the kind of numbers you'd need to keep the feline population down for generations. But given the panic, it's no wonder cat lovers are tempted to blame him for millions of plague victims. At the end of the day, people have loved their pets a lot, forever. It's a tough bond to break.

Nowadays, cats have resumed their comfortable perch in our homes—and atop our Halloween decorations, a lingering reminder of their witchy reputation. Also, we now have treatment for the bubonic plague, which is great.

BUBONIC PLAGUE LEADS TO MAJOR RAISES!

The bubonic plague claimed an unfathomable 75 to 200 *million* lives across the world, including one-third to one-half of the people in Europe alone. But a bit of good news for the people who were left: the Black Death eventually played a role in ending feudalism. For centuries, the social hierarchy of most of Europe had royals and nobility at the top, and peasants and serfs at the bottom. The lower classes had very few rights and extremely limited mobility, especially the serfs, who worked the land that nobles owned. Well, technically the king owned the land, but the nobles oversaw it, made a profit, and gave some of that profit to the king. The serfs, meanwhile, did all the work and got none of the money—they were simply allowed to live on the land that they cultivated. Basically an early version of a pyramid scheme, though not as early as the one that built the pyramids.

Before the plague spread, there were plenty of serfs. However, the bubonic plague decimated so much of Europe's population that by the time it had run its course, a serf's labor became a rare and valuable asset. How could a lord make any money with no one to till the fields? And what would happen if he couldn't pay the king? Peasants and serfs were suddenly able to negotiate, and they came out of those negotiations with better pay and better treatment.

This isn't to say that the class distinctions (or the class struggles) disappeared. But feudalism's neat little triangle was permanently damaged, and it fell apart not long after. Thanks, rats! (Or, thanks, fleas on rats!)

HYPNOSIS VS. MEDITATION AT THE WORLD CHESS CHAMPIONSHIP

There have been longer and tenser world championship chess matches, but perhaps none weirder than Karpov versus Korchnoi in 1978.

By the 1970s, chess had become one of many unusual fronts for the Cold War. Venerable grandmaster Viktor Korchnoi defected from the Soviet Union in 1976 over what he called "harassment and neglect by the Soviet chess federation." Two years later, he surprised everyone by qualifying for the World Championship at 47 years old, an age when many chess greats consider retirement. His opponent: defending champion Anatoly Karpov, a Soviet powerhouse twenty years his junior.

Petty mind games and paranoid squabbles dominated the three-month match. When Karpov's team brought him blueberry yogurt unprompted, Korchnoi's camp accused them of using the yogurt as a secret signal. Korchnoi donned a pair of reflective sunglasses; Karpov insisted that the glasses were meant to mess with him, and should be forbidden. After a particularly heated exchange of insults, Karpov refused to shake Korchnoi's hand. The two were no longer on speaking terms.

Korchnoi's greatest complaint: Karpov brought along a hypnotherapist, who fixed Korchnoi with a relentless, unnerving stare from the audience. Korchnoi believed (not unreasonably) that this was an intimidation tactic. He had defected from the USSR and could not be allowed to win. Korchnoi threatened to punch the hypnotist, then countered by inviting two yoga practitioners to meditate on his behalf as he played. His choice of guests was pointed: The peacefully meditating couple were fresh out of jail, found guilty of attempted murder. The press had a field day.

After months of questionably effective psychological warfare on both sides, Karpov prevailed, winning six games to Korchnoi's five. Their clash has been called "the dirtiest chess match in history." Hopefully they all took some time to meditate when it was over.

KARPOV

VS.

KORCHNOI

BIGFOOT BEGINNINGS

You've probably heard of Bigfoot—a large, hairy, humanoid creature that supposedly trudges through the American wilderness—and you might imagine he's some ancient myth or monster. He certainly invokes the image of the Yeti, which covers ground over the Himalayan mountain range. But you'd be wrong to link him to the prehistoric past.

Bigfoot, as we know him, came into existence less than a hundred years ago. The first report of Bigfoot was a letter in the *Humboldt Times*, a California newspaper, about a mysterious set of large footprints discovered by loggers. The newspaper printed the letter as a fun feature; to their surprise, it sparked reader interest, and journalists continued to write about the footprints and what type of creature could have made them.

Fascination eventually spread across the entire country, and there was even a thousand-dollar prize offered to anyone who could prove the creature's existence. Perhaps unshockingly, people started to come forward about Bigfoot sightings: grainy photos of big, hairy men, and tales of close encounters. Despite his shy, elusive reputation, Bigfoot became a media celebrity, a mainstay of adventure novels and monster movies; meanwhile, dubious documentaries claimed to be hot on his trail. Over

time, Bigfoot came to mean something more than himself—a symbol at once of nature's danger and its mystery, representing the need for humanity to treat the strange and wild with more respect. But despite his stardom, no one has ever provided conclusive proof that Bigfoot truly exists, or ever has existed.

So what are we to make of the photographs and footprints produced over the last fifty years? Some are definitively hoaxes; it turned out one infamous documentarian had just bought a gorilla costume and added some extra features. But the other, everyday sightings that leave hikers shaking—what are we to think of those? Joe Nickell, a cryptozoologist, offers the following explanation: What creature is large, hairy, walks on two legs with long swinging arms, and traverses the wilderness of northwest America and Canada? No, not Bigfoot, just an adult black bear, which often walks upright, lives in the exact same area, and is about the size of a larger-than-life human.

So if you're ever out in the woods and think you spot him, make sure you've got a camera, because that prize still hasn't been claimed. And bring some bear mace, too, just in case.

ANOTHER CRYPTID SPOTTED!

THE BIG MUDDY MONSTER

If you're looking for Bigfoot's extended family, and find yourself in Murphysboro, Illinois, you might be lucky enough to run into the Big Muddy Monster.

In the summer of 1973, a local couple spotted something frightening near Big Muddy River, a 156-mile-long (251 km) river with a mostly mud bottom that eventually joins the Mississippi. It wasn't Bigfoot, but it wasn't far off either. Standing before them was a 7-foot (2 m) monster covered in white hair and mud, with red eyes and yellow teeth. And it smelled absolutely awful. They stared at the creature, and for a moment it stared back before it eventually disappeared.

Police investigated, but couldn't find any ironclad proof that the monster was there. Despite this, officers reported that their dog picked up a scent, and followed a trail of strange slime to a spooky dead end.

Later, a traveling carnival reported an encounter that would add a new dimension to the creature. After the carnival closed for the night, four workers who handled the pony ride saw the animals suddenly panic. When the workers went to investigate, they came upon the monster hiding in the darkness. Although they, too, were afraid at first, they quickly noticed that the monster everyone feared appeared almost gentle. It stooped over the carnival ponies, admiring them for some time before escaping into the forest. As sightings continued, the mayor's office issued a statement encouraging residents to stay calm.

Knowing what you know about the Bigfoot hoaxes, you might think this was just someone playing an elaborate prank. But police, media, and residents agreed that couldn't be the case. The local newspaper editor, Tony Stevens, offered a practical reason it couldn't be faked: "This is hunting country, you know, and anyone who goes around in an animal costume is going to get his butt shot off."

While the original sightings sparked terror and later, confusion, the Big Muddy Monster is now a mascot. He's featured on the town mural and has his own yearly festival. Murphysboro recently unveiled a statue in his honor—a bronze, 800-pound (363 kg) recreation of the creature. Thankfully, they didn't try to recreate his smell.

Meet one more cryptid on page 109.

JOSEPH PUJOL: FARTISTE. FARTEUR. FARTISAN.

Paris, France. The early 1890s. The Moulin Rouge cabaret is packed, perhaps even at capacity, and the audience whispers excitedly. Somewhere in the crowd, the future King Edward VII of England is in attendance, unable to resist the rumors around tonight's act. Joseph Pujol takes the stage, and a hush falls over the theater. Joseph bows, prepares himself . . . and begins to fart.

Joseph Pujol was a *flatulist*, or professional farter, and performed under the stage name "Le Pétomane," which translates roughly to "The Fartomaniac." He had extraordinary control over his flatulence, and his show demonstrated the wide range of effects he could achieve.

He could imitate various musical instruments. Blow a candle out from several *feet* away. He could mimic cannon fire and a thunderstorm. He devised a rhyming story about a farm, interspersed with animal sounds made by, you guessed it, his butt. He could make a single fart a full ten seconds long.

Pujol first discovered his ability while swimming as a child—underwater, he tried holding his breath, inadvertently sucking water into his rectum at the same time. So much water got up his backside he had to go see a doctor, who thought it was kind of funny and told him to perhaps avoid the ocean. While initially frightened by this experience, Pujol later used his unusual powers to entertain his fellow soldiers during a stint in the army.

After Pujol left the armed forces, he worked as a baker in his hometown of Marseille, and wielded his artistic farts to amuse his friends and customers. Eventually he tried performing on the stage, surprising and delighting French provincial audiences; he met with so much success that he ended up traveling all the way to Paris, where he became a featured act at the Moulin Rouge.

It was a great arrangement for all involved. Pujol drew enormous sums of money to the world-famous cabaret, with box office sales that left other stage stars of the era in the dust. But he grew too big even for the Moulin Rouge, and Pujol took his fart act on the road for the next decade. Annoyed at losing their star performer, the manager of the Moulin Rouge sued Pujol for allegedly violating his contract. Pujol counter-sued the venue for their attempt to replace him with "La Femme Pétomane" ("The Female Fartomaniac"), who was quickly revealed to be faking her farts. He retired at the outset of World War I and returned to baking, but will always be remembered as a true fartiste.

The Dancing Mania, as depicted by Kendrik Hondius

THE DANCING PLAGUE OF 1518

One summer's day in 1518, Frau Troffea began to dance. There was no music in the streets of Strasbourg, yet she danced late into the night, unable to stop until she collapsed. The next morning, she began again, and a crowd gathered around her. Within days, the crowd grew, and dozens joined the spectacle, dancing themselves to exhaustion.

City officials in Strasbourg weren't sure what to make of the situation. They consulted the guild of physicians, who declared that the affliction would wear itself out. So the city built official stages and platforms to dance on, and brought in groups of musicians to play drums, strings, and horns to encourage dancing and speed along the dancers' recovery. But instead of the dance epidemic exhausting itself, it only exploded further. More onlookers joined in, as if by magnetic force. Within the month, hundreds of villagers were dancing uncontrollably, sometimes getting badly injured in the process.

The council tore down the stages, got rid of the musicians, and put serious limitations on dancing. All of the afflicted dancers were taken out of sight. There were some exceptions to the new rules—you could still enjoy yourself at, say, a wedding, as long as you only danced to stringed instruments. Drums were deemed too exciting, and no one wanted to encourage the mania that had already overtaken so many people.

People came up with a few different theories to explain this *choreomania*—a term for the uncontrollable urge to dance. At the time, many considered the "plague" to be a divine punishment for sin. This theory was bolstered when Frau Troffea and other dancing townspeople were healed at the shrine of Saint Vitus. Each dancer was given a small cross and red shoes before being sprinkled with holy water. After this treatment, the dancers finally stilled, and the plague that had lasted for over a month finally began to subside.

Physicians of the time agreed that early modern disco fever could be caused by sin, but also explained it as an imbalance of body humors. Humorism was an ancient medical belief that human bodies contain four types of bodily fluids that determine a person's temperament and health. According to this system, people get sick when the four humors—blood, yellow bile, black bile, and phlegm—are out of balance. Ever heard about doctors of the past using leeches to treat sick patients? That practice came from humorism. If a patient is suffering from too much blood, better get all that blood out of them. The physicians suggested that choreomania was caused by overheated blood, but rather than bust out the leeches, officials believed at first that the afflicted could simply dance it out of their system.

In modern times, some have suggested the urge to dance was caused by ergot poisoning, which can happen if you eat grain infected with a certain type of mold. However, while that poisoning can cause twitching and hallucinations, it also cuts off the blood flow to your legs until they lose function—no way could it cause the days-long dancing that infected onlookers. A more accepted theory is that the dancing was a form of mass hysteria caused by how stressful it was to be alive in 1518. After all, the plague didn't infect the wealthy or otherwise comfortable; it affected poor, working people who were hit hard by bad harvests and political instability. Plus, other instances of choreomania had broken out over the previous few hundred years, often during periods of great upheaval, and sometimes eased by prayers to Saint Vitus. In other words, people believed that this was something that could happen, and so it did. By engaging with that belief—that the dancing was divinely inspired, and that a saint could heal them—Frau Troffea, and everyone who danced with her, could finally put up their feet and rest.

The Tree That Owns Itself, Athens,
7306

THE TREE THAT OWNS ITSELF

It began as a legend, but now it's true: there is a tree in Athens, Georgia, that owns itself. The story goes back to August 12, 1890, when a local newspaper detailed one Colonel William H. Jackson's will, which gave the old oak tree on Jackson's land possession of itself as well as the land within 8 feet (2.5 m) of its trunk. Apparently Jackson had fond memories of the tree from when he was a child, and sought to protect it "for all time."

Can a tree *actually* own itself? Not really, at least not officially. But no one has challenged the tree's right of ownership; the public accepted the will as truth and has cared for the tree ever since. And it's easy to see why: the tree is an impressive sight. It stands 70 feet (21 m) tall and 3 feet (1 m) wide, cutting off traffic on the street where it lives.

Technically, the tree residing today on that patch of land is the first tree's heir. On October 9, 1942, the original tree, at a spry four

hundred years old, fell over during a storm. However, by that point, the tradition held a soft spot in Athens' heart, and the Junior Ladies Garden Club of Athens set out to replace the tree. They took acorns from the original site and began tending to a second–generation white oak. Four years later, they planted the sapling that now owns itself.

Today, the Junior Ladies Garden Club still cares for the tree, keeping it healthy and cleaning the property. If you choose to visit the site, you can find a plaque just at the edge of the tree's roots and read the legendary deed:

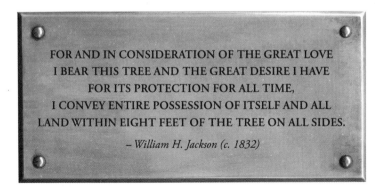

FOR AND IN CONSIDERATION OF THE GREAT LOVE
I BEAR THIS TREE AND THE GREAT DESIRE I HAVE
FOR ITS PROTECTION FOR ALL TIME,
I CONVEY ENTIRE POSSESSION OF ITSELF AND ALL
LAND WITHIN EIGHT FEET OF THE TREE ON ALL SIDES.

– *William H. Jackson (c. 1832)*

GREEN CHILDREN OF WOOLPIT

THEIR PARENTS BEING DEAD & GONE THE CHILDREN HOME HE TAKES

In the middle of the twelfth century, the fields of Woolpit, an ancient village in Suffolk, England, were usually quiet. Woolpit was named for the village's wolf pits, which trapped any wolves that might encroach on the settlement. But one day something different than wolves turned up in one of the fields, and the villagers were filled with fear. Out of the wilderness appeared two children. They spoke a language that no one could understand, they were dressed in unfamiliar clothes, and strangest of all, their skin was entirely green.

The villagers also noticed that the children were extremely nervous, and so the two were taken to the home of Sir Richard de Calne. He offered them food, but for days they refused. It seemed that they would not eat at all, until, upon finding some green beans in the garden, they ate ravenously, straight out of the ground.

The children lived with Richard de Calne for some time, and he was eventually able to get them to eat other foods. Eventually, due to the change in diet, their skin began to lose its green complexion. They also began to learn English. Seeking to understand the children's arrival, de Calne asked them where they came from, and how they got to England.

The answer they gave only added to the mystery. They spoke of a homeland that never saw sunrise or sunset, only a dim, cheerless twilight. It was not a description de Calne or the townspeople recognized.

When they explained how they got to Woolpit, they said that they were tending their father's flocks when they heard something not unlike church bells. They remembered listening to the chimes in admiration; they were entranced by the sound, and the next thing they knew, they were in England.

During their lifetime, the mystery remained unsolved. The boy died of an unknown illness not long after arriving at de Calne's estate. The girl, however, lived to adulthood. She eventually married, but the rest of her life is largely unknown.

There are a few different theories for the origins of this story. Some believe it's the retelling of an encounter between humans and mythical creatures, and that the children came from a place called Agartha, a legendary kingdom in the center of the earth. Others think that perhaps these children were aliens—after all, we do hear quite a few stories about "little green men" from Mars.

However, a likely explanation is that the children were simply Flemish refugees, who were persecuted at the time by King Henry II. (A different King Henry II than the one whose girlfriend liked to drink gold. More about her on page 68.) The unknown language they were speaking might have just been Flemish, a language the villagers of Woolpit would not recognize. This would also explain the unfamiliar clothes. As for the green skin, the fact that the color disappeared after some time and a change in diet suggests that they were simply malnourished.

Others suggest that the entire story is fictional, an allegory for otherness and for the changing landscape of England. Whatever the answer, all you need to know is this: If you are out catching wolves in a pit, bring gloves. And also, if you see two strange green children, make sure you have some beans on you, or at least directions to the nearest grocery store.

THE HORSE SHOE BEER FLOOD

Ninety-Nine Bottles of Beer on the Wall. Three Hundred Thousand Gallons of Beer in the Street.

On October 17, 1814, at 4:30 p.m., George Crick, a storehouse clerk at the Horse Shoe Brewery in London, England, was inspecting the vats when he noticed something out of place. On the wooden fermentation tank—nearly twenty-two feet tall and holding about 3,500 barrels' worth of porter—he saw that one of the 700-pound (318 kg) iron hoops had snapped off. The hoops were meant to stabilize the vat and hold it together.

A snap like this was not uncommon. Crick reported the issue to his boss, who told him to request a repair from another employee and then forget about it. For about an hour, Crick went on with his work. At 5:30, he heard the **boom**.

The vat had exploded, releasing ale with such force that it blew up some even bigger vats around it and broke through the back wall of the brewery itself. Beer flooded into the street at alarming speeds. More than 320,000 gallons swamped the neighborhood within minutes, destroying homes and killing citizens. Multiple newspapers reported on the destruction and chaos that followed. The brewery was built in St Giles, a poor, densely populated part of London, which meant that the explosion and flood did a lot of damage.

People could still smell beer in the streets for months following the flood. The disaster was ruled in court to be an "Act of God," meaning no one was responsible. The government even picked up the tab

The Horse Shoe Brewery

for some of the damages; the flood cost the brewery owners about 23,000 pounds ($28,000), which is about 1.25 million pounds ($1.5 million) today.

While the brewery was able to escape bankruptcy, they did stop using wooden vats, switching instead to significantly less explodable concrete ones. The Horse Shoe continued to brew beer at the same address for over a century, at least until London moved on from the idea of giant breweries right in the center of town. In 1922, the site was demolished, but at least this time it was on purpose.

ANOTHER UNUSUAL FLOOD

Just before the demolition of the Horse Shoe,

another strange and horrible flood struck, this time in Boston, Massachusetts. But it wasn't beer that spilled into the streets—it was molasses. When temperatures suddenly rose after a brutal cold snap in 1919, a giant steel tank burst, sending a two-million-gallon tidal wave of sweet and sticky liquid out of the warehouse at speeds of 35 miles per hour (56 km/h). (The phrase "slow as molasses" is so common you can find it in the dictionary, but the Great Molasses Flood flowed faster than the fastest human runner ever.) It killed twenty-one people and injured hundreds more, and locals say that the smell of molasses lingered in Boston for decades after the flood.

ANOTHER

ANOTHER

UNUSUAL FLOOD

Since apparently we are due for a weird flood every hundred years, the next struck in Lebedyan, Russia, in 2017. This time, fruit juice—apple, tomato, and orange, among others—soaked the town and flowed into the river after a warehouse roof caved in. Luckily, infrastructure has improved a lot over the past two centuries, and the event only resulted in two minor injuries. Who says the world isn't getting better?

THE LOST ART OF BARTITSU

In 1898, the gentleman engineer Edward William Barton-Wright returned from overseas to England and announced he'd created a new form of self-defense. He called it *Bartitsu*, which was a portmanteau (a word made up

from other words) of his own name (Barton) and jiujitsu, a form of martial arts he had studied while living in Japan.

Bartitsu was a unique combination of boxing, footwork, cane fighting, judo, and jiujitsu. Barton-Wright promoted his invention to the upper crust of Europe, calling it the "gentlemanly art of self-defense." At the turn of the century, sensational stories of stylish streetfighters appeared in newspapers across England.

These gentlemen were members of the Bartitsu Club, an "Academy of Arms and Physical Culture" where Barton-Wright held tournaments, presentations, and lessons. A magazine at the time described the club as "a huge subterranean hall, all glittering, white-tiled walls, and electric light, with 'champions' prowling around it like tigers." Barton-Wright hired experts in French kickboxing, walking-stick fighting, jiujitsu, fencing, Swiss wrestling, and good old fisticuffs to teach club members to fight and defend themselves. The academy also became the headquarters of a group devoted to Elizabethan-era swordplay—already antique at the time—

which led to the development of new stage-combat techniques. Shakespearean actors and Olympic fencers alike studied the blade at the Bartitsu Club.

The club attracted high-society members of London, including nobles and military officials. However, the cost of running such a complex operation far exceeded the number of people available and willing to pay high tuition costs or dedicate themselves for life to self-defense. The Bartitsu Club closed down in 1902, just four years after Barton-Wright began promoting his art.

Although the Bartitsu fad faded, Barton-Wright had kick-started an enduring public interest in martial arts. Former club instructors continued to teach and perform in "combat gymnasiums" in London and beyond. Some of these gyms and dojos became the first places to teach self-defense to women. Techniques from jiujitsu and cane-fighting (reimagined as parasol-fighting) helped suffragists protect themselves from intimidation and arrest while they protested for women's rights.

THE SUFFRAGETTE THAT KNEW JIU-JITSU.
The Arrest.

Bartitsu itself was saved from eternal obscurity by Sir Arthur Conan Doyle—notorious fairy investigator (see page 56) and the creator of *Sherlock Holmes*. In 1903, he published "The Adventure of the Empty House," in which Sherlock comes back to life after Conan Doyle killed him off in a previous story. When Sherlock describes to Watson how he survived a rooftop fight to the death with his nemesis, Moriarty, he acknowledges Bartitsu as his saving grace:

"We tottered together upon the brink of the fall. I have some knowledge, however, of baritsu, or the Japanese system of wrestling, which has more than once been very useful to me. I slipped through his grip, and he with a horrible scream kicked madly for a few seconds and clawed the air with both his hands. But for all his efforts he could not get his balance, and over he went."

Conan Doyle's story kept Bartitsu alive, albeit with an unusual spelling, for the next hundred years. In the early 2000s, the movement revived. The Bartitsu Society originated as an Internet fan group for Barton-Wright's old articles about Baritsu, and evolved into an organization devoted to his vision. Members of the association collected original works by Barton-Wright and his contemporaries to reconstruct the fighting techniques that original Bartitsu practitioners used. After publishing their findings in a compendium of classical Bartitsu, they committed to developing neo-Bartitsu, a blend of original and new techniques, to continue the project of collaborative learning from different schools of martial arts.

This research has been incorporated into film, television, literature, video games, and more. Modern Sherlock adaptations sometimes feature Bartitsu in their fight scenes, canes and all. So if you want to see the fighting in action, you don't have to go back in time, just turn on the TV. Or, if that's not up close enough, you can ask the Bartitsu Society for help starting your own neo-Bartitsu club (canes, swords, jiujitsu jackets, fencing helmets, boxing gloves, athletic cups, international team of experts, and two-volume *Bartitsu Compendium* not included).

BARRY MARSHALL, HUMAN PETRI DISH

Doctors Barry Marshall and Robin Warren were at a loss. Years of careful research were pointing them toward a simple treatment for painful stomach diseases. Even with proof that all their ulcer patients' guts were flooded with *H. pylori* bacteria, some of their colleagues dismissed or even ridiculed them for thinking the bacteria and the disease may be linked. Their experiments on lab mice weren't convincing anyone, their tests on pigs weren't working, and the path forward wasn't clear.

So Dr. Marshall took a fresh culture of *H. pylori*, dumped it in some broth, and drank it.

Three days later, he was nauseous and exhausted. His wife and coworkers noticed his breath smelled disgusting. An exam showed that his stomach lining was inflamed all over. He was well on his way to developing ulcers—holes in the stomach and intestines that cause burning pain and sometimes deadly complications.

This was, more or less, exactly what Marshall had hoped for.

Peptic ulcers are relatively common; up to 10 percent of people get them at some point in life. But until just a few decades ago, nobody knew they were caused by infections. Most doctors thought they knew why and how people got ulcers—for many years, they confidently blamed excess stomach acid, caused by stress, smoking, spicy food, or even someone's DNA. But Dr. Warren found that patients with ulcers had a type of unidentified bacteria in their stomachs. He shared this with Marshall, and the two made a hypothesis: if gastritis and peptic ulcers were caused directly by this bacterium, then ulcers could be treated with antibiotics! If so, the twentieth century's breakthrough medicine that saved countless lives could

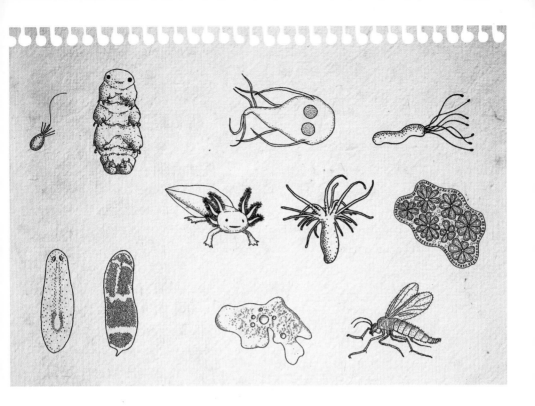

also help stop serious stomach diseases, surgical emergencies, and even cancer.

It took the team a while to even find the spiral-shaped bacteria they were looking for. It turned out that their first bacterial cultures hadn't had enough time to develop. The lab techs, busy and overloaded with a *Staph* infection outbreak, had thrown out the samples after just two days. By chance, one sample stayed in the lab over a long weekend and developed a lovely bunch of germs. The researchers got a second culture and found the shiny new bacteria they were after: *H. pylori*.

But the world of medicine was skeptical. Those bacteria were probably harmless, experts said. Reputation may have played a role, too; Marshall was young and unestablished, hailing from a remote mining town 300 miles (480 km) from the Western Australian coast, and Warren was "a little eccentric" and not always taken seriously by his peers. They needed concrete proof from human studies, and there was only one ethical way to do it. So Marshall drank his own bacteria, making himself a test subject. He even took an extra drug to make his stomach more infectable. He recovered with antibiotics, and the rest is history.

In 2005, twenty years after publishing their untraditional experiment, Marshall and Warren were awarded the Nobel Prize in Medicine for their discovery. Their message to the world: No matter how much we think we know, there's always more to learn.

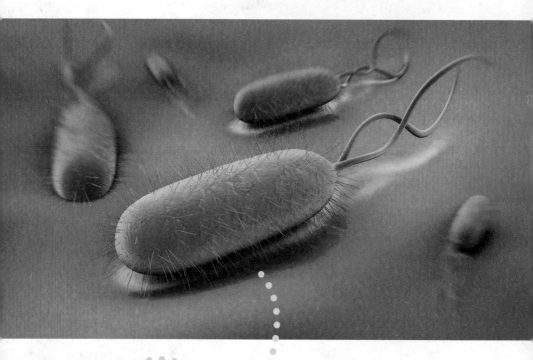

H. PYLORI

THE JERSEY DEVIL
OR, HOW BENJAMIN FRANKLIN'S WORK DRAMA INSPIRED A HOCKEY TEAM

He is the most American of monsters. He has been terrorizing the inhabitants of southern New Jersey unfortunate enough to meet him on the lonely Pine Barrens, for nearly 300 years. He has everything you could ask for in a demon: horns, wings, tail, a bloodcurdling shriek. Or maybe he's a flying kangaroo—accounts vary. He's the Jersey Devil: Official State Demon of New Jersey. And he owes it all to our turkey-electrocuting friend, Benjamin Franklin.

The Jersey Devil's tragic origin story has been kicking around since the 1700s, and it has many variations. Most involve a Quaker family named Leeds. Mrs. Leeds, known as "Mother Leeds," had twelve children when she became pregnant with her thirteenth. Amazingly, she was not overjoyed about this, and she may have spoken some unkind words to the tune of "let this child be a devil!" Depending on your version of the legend, she then either gave birth to a devil or a normal baby who immediately turned into one. After a mischievous rampage, he flew up the chimney and remains at large.

People began reporting regular sightings almost immediately and throughout the 19th century, sometimes from as far away as Philadelphia and farther afield in Pennsylvania. The hysteria reached fever pitch in 1909. Hundreds of people claimed attacks and other encounters, prompting hunting parties to comb the Pine Barrens

in search of the elusive beast. A famous hoax involved a dramatic capture and display of the monster—which turned out to be a kangaroo with fake wings fastened to its back. Lame, even by 1909 standards. Even the Piltdown Man (page 40) did it better.

The eerie landscape and remote location of the Pine Barrens may have contributed to the persistence of the Jersey Devil story. The flashing eyes of some creature on the parkway at night, strange hoofprints in the yard, a pathway through the marsh where dogs refused to go—with each report of something devilish, the panic added up. Many people, even today, staunchly claim that he exists, and warn the unwary about venturing onto the Pine Barrens. Rewards of up to $10,000 have been posted for the capture of the Jersey Devil (coincidentally not long before the kangaroo with wings turned up), but they remain unclaimed.

So where does Benjamin Franklin fit into all this? You could say that the Jersey Devil was born of a professional conflict that got out of hand. Back to the Leeds family—who were real people who actually existed. Daniel Leeds, husband to Mother and father to Devil, made his living as a pamphleteer and writer of almanacs, in direct competition to Benjamin Franklin's now-famous yearly publication, *Poor Richard's Almanack*. Leeds's writing leaned toward the occult, citing astrology. This upset the Quaker community and it broke with Leeds in 1690. Following Daniel Leeds's death, his son Titan took up the family business and went right on citing astrology and provoking both Franklin—whom he called a "fool" and a "liar"—and the Quakers. Rumors swirled about the Leeds family's association with witchcraft and the diabolical. The Leedses had made themselves very unpopular in southern New Jersey. Franklin did nothing to dissuade these rumors and was only too happy to keep them going to promote almanac sales. Leeds became conflated with Satan, and a monster was hatched, for real.

But what about hockey? If someone gave you a hockey team and you lived in New Jersey, what would you call it? In 1982 when the Colorado Rockies relocated to New Jersey, the state announced a contest to rename the team. The Jersey Devil(s) live on, on the Barrens, and on the ice. He even has his own theme song, written by New Jersey's favorite son, Bruce Springsteen: "A Night with the Jersey Devil."

SO WHAT IS IT, REALLY?

With no clear proof of a real live Jersey Devil, it's fair to wonder what people glimpsed in the Barrens that caused such a stir. One suspect, suggested by the head of a local Humane Society: a sandhill crane. They're about the Devil's height at 4 feet (1.2 m) tall, with mighty wings and a suitably bloodcurdling scream. These big birds are now plentiful in North American wetlands, and (like many humans in the northeast USA) they often travel through New Jersey on their way to somewhere else. But in the early 20th century, they were overhunted and their numbers were reduced, which could explain why the sight of one back then was so rare that a local wouldn't recognize it. Plus, almost anything would really scare you if it flew right past your windshield in the middle of the night. That said, the Sandhill Cranes isn't as good a name for a hockey team, so the legend of the Devil lives on as a source of local pride.

THE GREAT EMU WAR OF 1932—SOME TOUGH BIRDS

You've survived World War I. You're a hardened, seasoned warrior—a survivor. After the long, slow voyage back home to Australia, the government offers you free farmland in remote areas out west. They offer you financial assistance to grow wheat and other crops. Who wouldn't jump at the chance? Unfortunately, when making this decision, the Australian government fails to consider some of the environmental hazards of Western Australia: emus. This is going to be a problem.

Emus, large, flightless birds similar to ostriches, are creatures of habit. When they migrate, they take the same route, every time. They don't care if your farm is in their way. They were here first. They will eat most of your crops, trample the rest, and leave behind as much guano (poop) as you'd expect from a 75-pound (34 kg) bird.

To put it lightly, Western Australia is not suited to farming, as the farmers soon learn. As the global Great Depression looms and wheat prices tumble in the 1920s, the promised government aid somehow fails to arrive. You, farmer, war survivor, are poor, hungry, and pretty darn annoyed at how you're being treated after you've spent months

or years getting shot at on the front lines. The last thing you need is 20,000 emus showing up in your field to eat your livelihood. And yet that is exactly what happens. Apparently, emus find wheat delicious and irrigated fields a nice change from having to forage for water in dry Western Australia. And then the rabbits arrive. Hopping neatly through the holes kicked in the fences by their emu allies, they nibble away at whatever vegetation is left.

Australian settlers have a love/hate relationship with this iconic bird. Sometimes they're classified as a protected species; other times, vermin. The birds don't know or care—they're birds. In 1922, in an effort to assist the farmers in eradicating these pests, the Australian government reinstates the "vermin" designation. This turns out to be completely unhelpful, as the birds prove quite difficult to kill, even with firearms. Emus are heavily feathered; their hides are thick and leathery, and they are fast. Even the best marksman will have trouble hitting a moving target whose head is the size of a tennis ball.

You're enduring poverty and drought, and it's impossible to kill these bothersome birds who are bringing in all their rabbit buddies to cause further havoc. What's an Aussie to do? The farmers demand a military response, and they get one—kind of. Enter Major Gwynydd Purves Wynne-Aubrey Meredith, a man whose name could not possibly be made up. He and two other soldiers set out for Western Australia with a load of machine guns, to deal with this problem in a proper military fashion. This does not go as planned.

On November 2, 1932, Major Meredith (let's just go with that, OK?) and his aides recruit some local farmers to assist in rounding up the emus. Lucky for us, this is all being captured on film, as Meredith figures that his presumed resounding victory will make for great newsreel viewing.

As it turns out, emus are as resistant to herding as cats. The flocks immediately scatter across the surrounding landscape. An ambush at a local watering hole produces even worse results, as the machine guns jam, allowing the emus to escape. Pursuit by truck proves equally futile. As the Aussies grow ever more frustrated, the birds grow smarter, posting lookouts so their mates can munch uninterrupted or disappear into the Australian bush at the first sign of trouble.

The war continues in fits and starts for another month, producing around 986 emu casualties. *That's not even 5 percent!* The cost? 9,860 rounds of ammunition, and one truck that crashes after an emu's head gets stuck in the steering wheel. And through it all, the emus continue their march across Western Australia. Farmers persist in plugging away at the problem, but they're no match for the emus.

Following this, the Western Australia agricultural experiment gradually falls apart as farmers abandon the land that they cannot farm and the wheat that they cannot sell. Like many great historical failures before him, Major Meredith, the man who lost a war against a bird, is, of course, promoted, and ends his career as a brigadier.

After the emus win Meredith's Great Emu War, the farmers who stay behind eventually demand more ammunition, and the government offers bounties for each emu taken. This next wave of attacks is more effective, and the emu population takes a large hit. But public opinion shifts in favor of the emus—not only do many Australians find the idea of killing emus with machine guns horrifying, it's not a great use of resources either. As military tactics prove a poor longterm emu defense strategy, settlers turn to building massive fences that cut off migration, causing fears about the survival of emus and other Australian species. Conservation efforts build, and the emus have the last cackle: in 1999 they are once again declared a protected species. Maybe it's time to rethink the word "birdbrain."

VICTORIA, THE WORLD'S FIRST (ONLY?) KANGAROO TRAMPOLINE MODEL

Central Park in New York City, 1960. A man and kangaroo are hand in hand, waltzing and bouncing in time. George Nissen is a clever businessman, which is why he's in a three-piece suit. He's also an accomplished acrobat, which, oddly enough, is why he's dancing with a kangaroo. The two of them make a strange, amazing picture that earns worldwide fame for Nissen's game-changing invention: the trampoline.

It all began when Nissen was just 16, training hard in gymnastics and diving at his high school in Cedar Rapids, Iowa. One day, on a trip to the circus, he saw how trapeze artists safely practiced their high-flying acrobatics, leaping from great heights to land on a strong safety net far below. He wondered: What if, instead of a soft little bounce on the net, an athlete could spring all the way up again on the landing?

The idea enthralled him, and Nissen got busy trying to make a contraption with canvas and wood. He even took apart his bed to see if the bedframe would work. When he went off to college to follow his dream as a gymnast, his coach helped him develop the concept, adding iron, inner tubes, and eventually springs to make it bounce. Nissen brought his device to summer camp to practice with his fellow athletes, but he found out right away that the biggest fans of his new "bouncing rig" were kids.

Nissen loved sports, and at college he found out that he also loved math and science. He won multiple diving championships and earned a business degree. After graduation, he and his friends became traveling acrobats, living a low-paid but fun life on the road. They took their act to Mexico City, where Nissen learned the Spanish word for "diving board": *el trampolín*. He took the name home with him, and trademarked his bouncing rig under the name "Trampoline."

Inspired by how much the kids at summer camp had loved the trampoline, Nissen used both his business sense and his performance skills to market it to schools. Audiences loved it, but trampolines were large and new and complicated, so they only sold a few. When World War II hit, bringing hard times and metal shortages with it, Nissen thought that would be the end of the business. It turned out to be the opposite.

As young men joined the military in droves, the trampoline proved incredibly useful in training new pilots. The moments of weightlessness after the jump allowed recruits to practice reorienting themselves in midair. One pilot who went through trampoline training, Scott Carpenter, later became an astronaut who orbited Earth during the Mercury 7 mission. He and Nissen introduced trampoline training to NASA, where it became an important tool to prepare astronauts to go to space. Future astronauts practice defying gravity by playing "Spaceball" on a special triple trampoline.

Anyway, back to the kangaroo. Nissen was full of ideas to promote his invention, as you may have noticed by now. When the war was over, he wanted everyone to know the trampoline's potential. So he hatched a plan for a publicity photo that would demonstrate its bouncing power—starring one of the world's most famous jumpers.

Nissen found a guy out on Long Island who could get him a kangaroo. Her name was Victoria, and it cost Nissen $150 (about $1500 today) to rent her for a week. (The guy in Long Island had a more violent kangaroo available for $50, but Nissen wisely decided he'd rather shell out the extra $100.) He spent that week dodging her kicks and teaching her to bounce in sync with him. The photo he got in the end was a sensation, printed in papers worldwide. (Look it up, it's fantastic.)

Nissen's ultimate ambition was to get the trampoline into the Olympic Games. He lived to see it happen, at the 2000 Summer Olympics in Sydney, Australia. He was invited to test-bounce the Olympic trampoline before the competition, and he eagerly did, at the nimble young age of 86. Trampoline has been a permanent part of Olympic gymnastics since then, and does it say anywhere in the rules that a kangaroo can't compete?

AGENT GARBO, THE SELF-EMPLOYED SPY

Juan Pujol García was a small, unassuming man, a Spaniard living in Madrid during the early stages of World War II. He had fought in the Spanish Civil War, but avoided the front lines and claimed to have never fired a single shot during his service. His college degree was in animal husbandry.

He was also among the most skilled and successful spies of the Second World War, and played a vital part in ensuring the success of the D-Day invasion and the eventual victory of the Allied forces in Europe.

García was not recruited to be a spy, however. In fact, he contacted the British embassy in Madrid three separate times in 1941, requesting to be trained as a spy for the British intelligence agency, MI5. His request was denied all three times, and for most people, this would have been the end of the story—but not for the man who would eventually be known as Agent GARBO.

Unfazed, García decided he'd become a spy with or without MI5. He contacted the Germans, claimed to be a zealous believer in the fascist cause, and told them he wanted to spy on Britain for the Nazis. They trained him in basic espionage and instructed him to travel to England, where he was to build up a network of contacts that could gather intelligence for Germany.

But truthfully, Juan Pujol García despised fascism following his service in the Spanish Civil War, and never had any intention of staying loyal to the Nazis. He was a double agent from the very beginning. The side he was really working for had no idea what he was up to, but that didn't bother him at all.

García got to work. He crafted an intricate network of contacts and sub-agents: each and every one of them completely imaginary. Using travel guides and reference books, he wrote and delivered detailed reports about different parts of the UK. Impressively, he did this without ever actually setting foot in England, working entirely from Lisbon, Portugal.

When García next got in contact with British intelligence, he had connections in Germany and a credible cover as a Nazi agent, plus a big network of made-up contacts he could pretend to double-cross without endangering any real agents. Unsurprisingly, Britain was eager to hire him this time around.

García—now with the codename "GARBO"—had even more success with the help of his new MI5 handler, Tomás Harris. Together, they expanded and elaborated on his imaginary contacts, crafting entire identities and life stories for them. Altogether, they created 27 such characters, which helped convince Nazi officers of García's credibility.

Now backed officially by the British, Agent GARBO began giving Germany information about actual military operations. These reports had to be carefully timed so as not to endanger the operations in question. They were postmarked earlier than they were sent, and arrived too late to be of any use to the Germans. But the information itself was convincing, and the Nazis continued to trust him.

Now that Agent GARBO had them wrapped around his finger, it was time for his most important job yet: to help ensure the success of D-Day and the Normandy landings, which began on June 6, 1944.

The landings at Normandy were planned by American and British forces, under the codename Operation OVERLORD. The Axis powers suspected that the Allies would attempt an invasion by sea, but didn't know their precise landing spot. The success of OVERLORD depended on keeping this crucial detail a secret. Agent GARBO's mission was to misdirect the Germans and point their attention to a fake invasion.

It was what all of GARBO's work had led up to. Every fake contact and sub-agent, every carefully timed leak of information, every report and bit of communication was to set the stage for this deception.

Agent GARBO sent his most important reports yet. The soldiers storming the beaches in Normandy, he warned, were nothing more than a diversion, meant to distract the Germans while the Allies launched their real invasion further up the coast of France. García reported 11 army divisions—150,000 soldiers, led by a formidable U.S. general—poised to strike in the far north at Pas-de-Calais. No such army existed.

The deception worked. For the next three months, instead of sending all their forces to Normandy, Germany kept hundreds of tanks and hundreds of thousands of men behind to protect Pas-de-Calais from an attack that never came. The Allied land invasion of France succeeded, and eventually the war was won.

Throughout all of this, Nazi Germany remained convinced that Juan Pujol García was a trustworthy, loyal asset. Completely oblivious to his real role in D-Day, they awarded him the Iron Cross just two months later, a medal normally given to soldiers and never to spies. Later that same year, García was also made a member of the Most Excellent Order of the British Empire, an honor usually reserved for British citizens. He's one of the only people to receive awards from both sides of the Second World War.

All this to say: Even if the odds look small, try dressing for the job you want, not the job you have.

THE MAGICAL MERMAIDS OF WEEKI WACHEE SPRINGS

They're gorgeous and graceful. They glide through the water with an elegance that enchants anyone fortunate enough to catch a glimpse of their aquatic dance. Who are they? They're manatees, of course!

Between the romantic idea of meeting a mythical creature, the manatee's undeniable charm, and the fact that lots of people go a little nuts at sea, it's understandable how sailors mistook these gentle marine mammals for mermaids. Legends of mermaid sightings abound, dating back to the Age of Exploration (Christopher Columbus and his crowd), and even turn up in tales from ancient Babylon and Greece. If you spotted a sea creature that you couldn't identify—one that could turn its head with humanlike curiosity, or hold things with the fingerlike bones in its flippers—you might think you saw a mermaid.

Native to warm waters throughout the world, manatees (although they're threatened by human activity) are a familiar sight in Florida's waterways, frequenting the many clear, warm freshwater inland rivers and springs. One coastal haven they visit is Weeki Wachee Springs in western Florida, whose name is Seminole for "little spring" or "winding river." It's unique in the crystal clarity of its waters, its refreshing temperature, and a strong current that flows from the deepest underground spring in the U.S.

But in the 1940s, some people saw Weeki Wachee Springs as a place to dump unwanted junk and household objects. Newton Perry saw something different: a paradise swimming with mermaids.

Perry, nicknamed "the Human Fish," was a stunt swimmer in movies and TV. He could even ride a bicycle underwater! While working as a stunt double in a Tarzan film, Perry invented an air hose that connected to a compressor, freeing the diver from the need to carry a scuba tank on their back.

In 1947, Perry decided to combine his super-swimmer skills, showbiz experience, and love of the Florida springs and use them to produce a mermaid show. After rounding up investors and dredging Weeki Wachee Springs of human-made debris, Perry constructed an underwater theater below the springs' surface, right into the surrounding limestone rock, so that 18 audience members could view the show up close.

Feeding the Ducks at Colorful Weekiwachee Spring On U. S. #19, near Brooksville, Fla.

THE UNDERWATER THEATRE

The theater's designers cleverly hid the air hoses in the scenery. Perry recruited athletic young women to be his "mermaids" and trained them to use the air hoses to appear as if they weren't using any kind of breathing tube at all. The mermaids frolicked 20 feet (6 m) below the surface of the natural spring, swimming in choreographed ballets, acting out scenes from popular films, playing games, and even having picnics, all underwater.

And this was no easy feat. These women had to be incredibly strong swimmers to perform flawlessly against the underwater current. Mermaids receive months of training on land before ever donning their mer-tails and taking the plunge.

The mermaids were an immediate hit. In 1959, ABC Television purchased the springs and enlarged the theater to 400 seats; by the 1960s, up to 35 mermaids lived and worked at the Springs. Their flowing acrobatics thrilled tourists with eight shows every day. As time passed, the park added more attractions like a petting zoo and a birds-of-prey exhibit that specialized in rehabilitating wildlife. And yes, they added mer-men too! They're called "princes."

Today, Weeki Wachee Springs belongs to Florida's State Park System. The mermaid shows have been enhanced with sound and special effects, still delighting crowds. And, if you take a quiet kayak ride down one of the many channels, you may just be lucky enough to spot the original mermaids—manatees.

Many mermaids first got their fins as teenagers, but it's not just a young fish's game. Vicki Smith got the job fresh out of high school in 1957; back then, there were only two underwater hoses in the spring, the pay was about $3 per show, and they had to watch for hand signals from park employees to warn them of any snakes or gators visiting the spring. (Today there are underwater sound systems and a personal hose for each mermaid.) More than 60 years later, Smith was once again swimming, somersaulting, and drinking underwater soda pop with the Legendary Sirens, a group of veteran Weeki Wachee mermaids in their 60s and 70s.

MYTH OR MAMMOTH?

Around 440 BCE, the ancient Greek historian Herodotus wrote about a war between two city-states, Sparta and Tegea. After a string of rough losses, the Spartans asked for wisdom from the Oracle of Delphi. Delphi was a sacred site where many ancient Greeks went for help when they had to make important decisions.

The oracle priestess replied with a prophecy: In order to win, the Spartans would have to find the bones of Orestes, the son of a legendary king who battled in the Trojan War, and bring them back to Sparta. In typical prophecy fashion, the oracle offered only a vague hint about the bones' location: a place "where winds are forced to blow, and a strike is answered by a strike." Confusing!

But then, a Spartan soldier got word that a metalsmith in Tegea found some weird enormous bones in a weird enormous coffin while trying to dig a well near his smithy—a place where winds are forced to blow (using a device called a bellows, for stoking the fire), and a strike is followed by a strike (a loud hammer hitting a loud anvil). The soldier sneaked off to Tegea, snagged the huge bones, and brought them back to Sparta.

The coffin was allegedly about 10 feet (3 m) long—those would be some BIG human bones. But that only bolstered the Spartans' belief that these were the bones of the prophecy. The Trojan War was already an ancient legend by the time these Spartan soldiers were around, and they believed that heroes of the past would have been much bigger than humans in their own time. Herodotus wrote that Sparta did go on to win the war with Tegea, and the city-state became a major power in the centuries that followed. Prophecy complete, case closed.

UNLESS...

Herodotus, though he's known to have included (many!) exaggerations and tall tales in his Histories, wrote a lot of things that have helped modern scholars understand the ancient world. Even when something in his work can be disproven as a fact, that discovery can still lead to an amazing insight when combined with other things we've learned in the last 2,500 years. And a few scholars, like the Irish professor George Huxley and American researcher Adrienne Mayor, have a theory for why giant bones could have turned up in the blacksmith's backyard.

The ancient territory of Tegea lay across a prehistoric lake basin, home to the remains of mammoths and other Ice Age mega-mammals. Huxley and Mayor suggest that long before Herodotus, even before the war between Sparta and Tegea, someone discovered the bones of a big extinct creature from the Pleistocene era. Since they'd heard of ancient heroes but hadn't heard of mammoths, they arranged them into a human shape and gave them a respectful burial. Generations later, someone else dug up the coffin and made some pretty understandable assumptions. Then that story made it to Herodotus, and eventually made it all the way to us, in a long game of prophecy telephone.

So what do the thousands of years' worth of stories in this book, from Gilgamesh to Goncharov, have in common? People tell stories to help make sense of the world—or to make it even weirder. We use them to admire others' accomplishments and to inspire our own. Sometimes we tell them so we can laugh at the crazy things people really believed back then—even though we don't know how much of what we accept as fact today will look just as ridiculous when people many years from now look back at us. As we continue our never-ending quest for knowledge, we learn again and again that it's our creativity, cleverness, and just plain weirdness that make us human. Look for that in every story, and you're sure to find it.

ADDITIONAL CREDITS
Certain images in this book were used under the following Creative Commons licenses.